Early pr

"Over the years ou~~r~~
Rosa Sailes' ability to ~~encourage people to~~
Holy Spirit in their journeys of faith. Because that same level of insight and wisdom flows through Let *Her Life Speak*, readers have new opportunities to embrace the lives of these biblical heroines through this transformative and refreshing devotional study."

~*Dr. Byron T. Brazier*
Pastor of the Apostolic Church of God

"*Let Her Life Speak* encourages the reader to redefine the lives of these female biblical figures. The compelling truth is that the Rachels and Rahabs of yesterday are a real reflection of the Robins and Ritas of today. As you journey through the tapestry of history, holding the hands and feeling the hearts of these biblical women, *Let Her Life Speak* will become an essential to your biblical studies."

~*Rev. Carolyn Butler*
Regional Director of Christian Education
Pentecostal Assemblies of the World

"If you would like a deeper relationship with God, Let *Her Life Speak* is a 'must-read' publication that will challenge you to see seven Old Testament women from a different perspective. It will stimulate your mind through discussions and inspire you to speak to your realities. This thought-provoking, inspirational, and stimulating book will be an asset to anyone who sincerely desires to deepen their search for women in the biblical text and rethink how that research addresses women on the church today."

~*Rev. Dr. Sandra Smith*
President of Rhema Word Ministries

Let Her Life Speak

What the Lives of Women in the Bible Say Today

Enjoy & be blessed.

Rosa Sailes

ROSA SAILES, Ed.D., M.T.S.

Printed in the United States of America

ISBN 9780985465490

Publisher: Keys to the Kingdom Publishing, LLC
P.O. Box 2812
Bristol, CT 06011
1-800-912-6282
www.ktkpublishing.com

Scripture taken from the King James Version, New International Version®, NIV®. Copyright © 1973, 1978, 1984, 2011 by Biblica, Inc.™ Used by permission of Zondervan, New Living Translation, copyright © 1996, 2004, 2015 by Tyndale House Foundation. Used by permission of Tyndale House Publishers Inc., Carol Stream, Illinois 60188. All rights reserved., and the New King James Version®. Copyright © 1982 by Thomas Nelson. Used by permission. All rights reserved.

Cover Design by Trinidad Zavala

Library of Congress Control Number: 2016939855

I offer this book to God, who gives me strength and whose Grace has blessed me beyond anything I could have imagined.

⁓

I dedicate this volume with love and thanks to my mother, Bessie Jordan, who taught me to know God; and to the memory of my husband, Michael Sailes, who passed away as this book was being finalized for publication. His faith that God had gifted me to encourage others through teaching, preaching, and writing exemplified his faith in God and his love for me. His care and patience gave me the space and encouragement to write and will forever undergird my work for the Lord.

Contents

Foreword

A FEW YEARS AGO after speaking at a campus event on biblical perspectives on women's leadership, a young woman approached me. She was both intrigued by my presentation and somewhat intimidated by the subject matter. You see, she had been raised in a church whose leaders had an ultra conservative view on women's leadership in the church. Women, in their view, were not allowed to be pastors, ministers or teachers of men. Women were restricted to teaching children and other women.

She now learned that there were women in the Bible who God used to lead others, both men and women. The lives of these women spoke to the core of this young woman's life. She was sensing a calling into ministry from the Lord and experiencing such great freedom in her campus ministry organization, yet the teachings of her childhood church nagged at her. What she was experiencing was echoed in the lives of women leaders in Scripture such as Deborah, Miriam, Esther, and Lydia. Their lives as leaders spoke to this young woman grappling with her call to leadership.

What this young woman discovered through my seminar and our ensuing talk is that the lives of women in Scripture speak to us to today. Today, through this wonderful book, Dr. Rosa Sailes reinforces this same message. Dr. Sailes provides a perspective on women in Scripture that is insightful, thought-provoking, and sometimes quite provocative.

From her opening chapter on Bathsheba to the final one on Ruth, Dr. Sailes asks questions of the text to which women of today can relate. No doubt some of you have asked some of these same questions about your own lives, but were not quite sure where to get answers. Dr. Sailes raises issues that are relevant, and her answers from the text are revelatory.

Each chapter is dedicated to a particular woman of Scripture. The women chosen are not always the women most read about in Scripture. For each woman presented, Dr. Sailes does a painstaking analysis of this woman's life, providing the historical and cultural context that brings her story to life. Then Dr. Sailes provides an interpretive perspective that provides meaning to this woman's life, but also demonstrates to us the value God placed on this woman by including her story in the writ of Scripture.

Finally, for each woman's story, we the readers are invited to join the dialogue to ask our own questions about what we will do as a result of this sacred encounter. Using the biblical woman's story as a launch pad, Dr. Sailes leads us to an inquiry into the meaning of our own lives and women's lives in general. And we are challenged to change and be change agents. From the dicey dynamics of power and seduction in the ancient world, we are forced to pause and consider those same questions for women today. From the humiliation of being cast aside for another woman, we are compelled to consider the coping strategies we use for rejection today. From the specialness of safe places for women written about in a couple of places in Scripture, we are encouraged to create our own safe places. This book and the dialogue that ensues will encourage real conversation and real action.

Dr. Sailes reminds us that women have always been and still are important to God. No matter what we go through, we matter to the Lord. Through pain and sorrow, to challenges and changes, God cares. The issues change in nuance across time, but the issues are so fundamental to womanhood that the lives of each woman that Dr. Sailes writes about speaks to our very core as women. No better person can write about such life-filled stories as Dr. Sailes, whose own life has spoken to many and made a difference.

I remember when I first arrived in Chicago fresh out of graduate school and was settling into my new church home, the Apostolic Church of God. Dr. Sailes was the leader of the Christian Education department we called Sunday Morning Bible Study. She asked me to teach an elective course. I asked her what might be appropriate topics for such an elective course. Without hesitating, she said, "develop a Bible study course around your passions." My passions were (and still are) women's empowerment and leadership development. So I developed a Bible study course on women's leadership. Dr. Sailes's encouragement was the catalyst for a class at our church, many workshops and national presentations, and my first published book, *Leading Ladies: Transformative Biblical Images for Women's Leadership*.

Now it gives me great pleasure to read, support, and advocate on behalf of *Let Her Life Speak*. Dr. Sailes picks up where *Leading Ladies* left off. Not only has God given witness in Scripture to using women in leadership, but God also gives witness through the lives of women in Scripture that our stories, our experiences are not peripheral or incidental to Him. Dr. Sailes gives us the lens through which to see the intentionality of God's concern and care for women of antiquity and by extension women of today.

May you be blessed as you read *Let Her Life Speak*, and may this book give you the courage to let your own life speak.

Dr. Jeanne Porter King
Author, Ministry Leader, Inspirational Speaker
President, TransPorter Group Inc.

Appreciation

This book could not have been completed without the support of numerous people including the members of my family who always believed that my words could help others: my brothers and sisters; Antoine and Linda Joyce Jordan, Frank and Linda Faye Jordan, and Johanna Jackson; my aunt, Julia Clark; and my cousin Lorna Hudson.

I greatly appreciate the "children" God gave me to strengthen me in this journey: Terrence Hargrove, who encouraged me to complete this book; Patrice Wilbur and Richard Gano, who always found ways to help me get beyond my own doubts.

I thank God for the women who have prayed me through as my co-laborers in ministry: Jeanne Porter King, Alice Kinnard, Carolyn Butler, JoMarie Cooper, Sandra Smith, Sharon Harrison, Barbara Martin, Sylvia Franklin, Lori Caesar, Sarah Martin, Gwendalyn Blair, Jennifer LuVert, Granada Cartwright, Ivory Nuckolls, Marcella Simmons, and Aja Carr-Favors.

I especially give thanks and credit to the women whose participation in the classes I've taught, contributed to my understanding of the importance of this book.

What My Life Spoke

FOR MANY YEARS I have taught the Bible to men and women, teens and adults. While my classes, workshops, and seminars often addressed gender, I seldom centered on women's issues. Naturally, how the Bible refers to women and the cultures in which biblical persons are represented was important, but focusing on the woman's perspective was not usually central for me. In fact, it seldom seemed central to the text. But then God changed things.

I found myself questioning how the lives of women in the Bible are relevant to women today. The cultures seemed so different that women appeared to be secondary to the passage of study. Even when women were a deciding factor or the most critical figures in the text, they managed to end up in the "back seat." I found, however, that when I began to dig deeply, the lives of women in the

Bible spoke to me. I became increasingly sensitive to their histories and their plights. I sought to understand their world and their struggles in it.

And God kept changing things. I found myself developing sermons and Bible studies that centered on women in the Old and New Testaments. I was also called upon to teach several women's classes and retreats. The women in attendance were inspired to hear what the lives of women in the Bible were saying to them. They appreciated the encouragement these biblical voices spoke to their faith. With that, this book was born.

Let Her Life Speak is a Bible study tool developed primarily (but not solely) for women. It is a devotional text that emphasizes the application of the Bible for spiritual growth. While the research incorporates the work of Bible scholars, the emphasis is always on helping women embrace the Bible for daily living. *Let Her Life Speak* is written with the understanding that the Bible is the Word of God. Several translations are used to clarify the text, but the veracity of Scripture is always stressed. With that in mind, *Let Her Life Speak* presents the Bible as spiritual truth that speaks to our hearts and minds in order to challenge our assumptions about women in the Bible and our actions as followers of Christ.

Each Bible woman in this book is highlighted in a "discussion." I chose this term (rather than "chapter") because I believe that through the lives of the people in the Bible, God speaks to us and invites us to respond. The women in this volume are popular Old Testament figures. Several have been mentioned in sermons but may not have been examined closely. *Let Her Life Speak* magnifies the cultures, relationships, and spiritual awakenings of these Bible women in order to encourage discussion about what their lives have to say to Christian women today.

Each discussion includes commentary and reflective exercises. The commentary has five sections:

Scripture – Each discussion begins by identifying key Bible passages that reference the woman whose life is being discussed.

Synopsis – This is a recap of the biblical narrative that connects the events, situations, and people in the woman's life. The result is a tapestry of her Bible presence that focuses on the actions of the people rather than an analysis of God's actions.

Life in Her World – This section of the discussion examines the political, economic, religious, and social factors at work in this woman's era. It considers the interplay of nations, customs, religious practices, and family relationships as a backdrop of that woman's experiences.

God in Her Life – Each discussion searches for the woman's engagement with God. Women's God-encounters are seldom directly mentioned in the text. Thus, this analysis looks for the subtle references to God's presence and power in the background of events or the fiber of the woman's personal or family life.

What Her Life Speaks – At the core of this book are the spiritual concepts we learn from these women's lives and their encounters with the Almighty God. Through these concepts, we see where biblical lives touch the reality of life today.

Each discussion ends with two reflective sections that allow you to add your voice and extend the conversation.

What Your Life Speaks – This first reflective component asks you to "Speak Your Truth" as you contemplate the concepts discussed in that Bible woman's life. Focus Your Faith asks you to consider how you can make the spiritual connection between your faith journey and what you have gleaned from the study of that Bible woman.

Using Your Voice – The second reflective section begins with Ponder and asks you to engage a spiritual practice or a faith question. This activity aims to encourage your continued study of the Bible and strengthen your relationship with God. Pray encourages you to formulate prayers based on both your concerns and the issues raised in the discussion. Practice suggests strategies and activities that address the life issues suggested by the discussion.

As you read these accounts of biblical women, I pray the Holy Spirit will challenge your thinking. I hope you will let go of the usual treatments and interpretations of Bible women and the events that occurred with and around them. It may be that your original view has merit and is filled with truths that encourage your faith. Even then, I urge you to make room for different perspectives. Let your examination of these women grow from a fresh look at God's Word through their eyes so that you may see your own faith journey in a new light. As you enter this discussion with heart and mind, you will understand even more clearly what God is speaking to your life through the lives of these Bible women.

Listening to Bible Voices with Heart and Mind

THE BIBLE IS THE WORD OF GOD, and *Let Her Life Speak* is written with the understanding that studying the Bible strengthens our spiritual walk. Unfortunately, many Bible studies fail to glean spiritual truths from the lives of women in the Bible as readily as they search for meaning in the lives of men in the Scriptures. A primary goal of *Let Her Life Speak* is to increase the instances when Christians connect positively to the circumstances surrounding women in the Bible. For example, how often do you think of women in the Bible as whole people? How likely are you to think of women in the Bible as examples of manipulative individuals, bad behavior, or invisible foils for male adventures? How often do narratives about women in the Bible serve as encouragement for your daily living?

We seek to know God's Word because it is "alive and powerful. It is sharper than the sharpest two-edged sword, cutting between soul and spirit, between joint and marrow. It exposes our innermost thoughts and desires" (Hebrews 4:12 NLT). To embrace the lives of women in the Bible as sources of spiritual encouragement, we must consciously read the Bible with hearts (emotions) and minds (knowledge and intellect). When we do this, the individuals in the Bible become people who speak to us from the pages of God's Word. Since there are many women in the Bible, this goal seems simple. But there are several reasons why most Christians give little attention to these women.

First, many of the best-known Bible women have been popularized through movies. Bathsheba, Esther, and Delilah are examples of biblical reference "characters" who have endured through pop culture. While many of these movies have been financially successful, they often have no relationship to the biblical narrative—except for the names of their main characters. Anyone who learns the Bible through the lens of Hollywood or independent production companies gets an impression that is often skewed or inaccurate. For example, the 1960 film *Esther and the King* showed Esther as a young woman engaged to a warrior in the king's army. Queen Vashti was depicted as a villain who spitefully crashed the king's banquet and performed a lewd dance that ended with her standing naked before the king and his entire court. Movies about David and Bathsheba generally portray these two amazingly beautiful people in a love story that ignores the tension in their relationship and the sin at the base of their encounter. Hollywood films provide a fleeting attraction to the love story, but they fail to give us any real knowledge about human nature or God. Because appropriating Bible truths requires faith on the part of the reader, many of the most popular Bible movies today resort to theatrical insertions to "fill in the blanks" for viewers when faith seems too far-fetched for the script. Therefore, we remember the full-screen caricatures but make no personal or spiritual connection to the biblical events.

The second reason people do not connect with Bible women (and men) is connected to a staple of church teaching. Sunday school and its many derivatives (Vacation Bible School and denominational youth Bible programs) were started to provide biblical knowledge, moral lessons, and reading skills to children. Today, depending on the age group, Bible lessons for children are sterilized to be palatable for young participants. In these contexts, David never met Bathsheba and Sampson fought but never shed blood. Because Sunday school lessons only focus on a few individuals, accounts of selected figures (usually male) may be repeated in the same year or cycle with only a change in the Scripture reference. Compounding these problems is the fact that fewer parents take their children to Sunday school, which means that fewer children are available to even learn who is in the Bible. Sunday schools and other Christian education programs have long included adult and teen classes. However, teens and young adults are growing more reluctant to attend congregational Bible lessons because they see no substantive value in these Christian education programs.[1]

Third, there is a lack of awareness about the women (and men) in the Bible because most Christian education programs are conducted by lay persons with little, if any, training in theology and instructional approaches. When instructors are not able to energize Bible lessons with rich content and strategies, Bible studies leave readers with one-dimensional, fictionalized "characters" in nice "stories" that dilute the importance of God in the human experience. When the history of the Bible is neglected, there is little room to explore the diversity of nations or people presented in the biblical narratives. Moral lessons may be extracted, but the Bible becomes increasingly disconnected from the realities of daily life.

When the hearts and minds of people are not engaged, they recall Bible events as "fairy tales" that lack power and deny the relevance of God in human life today. When teachers include the background of Scripture texts, they help learners make a connection between two worlds—biblical and modern. When studies examine women in the Bible in the context of their social and cultural situations, there is an opportunity to develop a meaningful connection with current events and learners' lives. This connection then triggers an emotional response through the memory of the learners' experiences. Even though readers' experiences may be very different from the events in the Bible narrative, learners engage in personal and spiritual reflection in ways that movies and congregational teaching attempt but often fail to achieve.

Let Her Life Speak will take readers on a journey of reflection (heart) and exegesis (mind). Exegesis is the process of combing through the Bible text for fresh nuggets of meaning. Reflecting on what we learn, creates a bridge between the experiences of women in the Bible and women today. This bridge creates a spiritual connection that transcends time and space. For example, when the Bible person under study is depicted as a flat or one-dimensional character, reading a Bible narrative that involves the death of her child will garner a sympathetic response from the reader. The facts will be understood, but sorrow for the character will only create a narrow sensitivity to her situation. The encounter will lack the strength to touch the reader's heart in ways that ask, "Lord, what does this say to my situation?" On the other hand, if the life of the Bible woman is explored in the context of her world, the reader sees her as a multi-faceted person and is drawn into her situation. Now the reader becomes empathetic, fully immersed in the biblical woman's emotional pain. With this context, even though the reader may have never experienced that situation, she is compelled to examine her own life and ask for God's direction and help.

When we read the lives of Bible women with hearts and minds, we go beyond the printed narrative to examine the socio-political world of the Bible. We are free to peek into biblical lives and relationships. We begin to listen closely for the voices in and through the text as well as the implications surrounding the events. When we listen to Bible voices with hearts and minds, we explore Bible women's perspectives of God's divine presence and find that their lives call us to dig more deeply into God's Word and more honestly into our own lives as we extend the discussion for ourselves.

Bathsheba

2 Samuel 11; 2 Samuel 12, 1 Kings 1

Synopsis

When we select the best love stories ever, David and Bathsheba surely make the top ten. Like most romances that move from the Bible to the big screen, we soon find that there is a little more hype and a lot more drama than the original account. When we set the scene as the Bible does, we learn that the battle between Israel and the Ammonites was raging when David first laid eyes upon Bathsheba. The Bible says that it was spring, the season when kings go to war (2 Sam 11:1). David was a warrior-king. His reputation as a warrior began when he was too young to enlist in Saul's Army but decided to battle Goliath—and won (1 Sam 17). For his entire adult life,

David was at war. However, on this particular day, David was home napping on the roof of his home. It was after a nap, probably in the late afternoon or early evening, that he saw Bathsheba bathing. From the roof of his home, the king had a view of the entire city. His gaze, however, focused on Bathsheba—"a woman washing herself; and the woman was very beautiful to look upon" (2 Sam 11:2).

The answer to David's inquiry regarding the woman's identity would have stopped most men cold; but then David was not most men. Bathsheba's grandfather was Ahithophel, one of David's chief advisors (1 Chron 27:33; 2 Sam 23:34). Bathsheba was the wife of Uriah, who, like her father, Eliam, was listed among David's "Thirty Mighty Men" (2 Sam 23:39). The men in Bathsheba's family were not just soldiers in the army or servants at the court. They were leaders who were well-known by and loyal to David. Despite Bathsheba's relationship to his most trusted aides, David pursued his advantage and had Bathsheba brought to his home and into his bed. When Bathsheba later revealed that she was pregnant, David set in motion a series of incidents that compounded his sin.

In an elaborate effort to create a cover-up, David had Bathsheba's husband Uriah brought home from the battlefront. Despite David's affirmation in 1 Sam 21:5 that he did not permit his men to have sexual relations when they were engaged in battle, the king hoped that the battle-weary soldier would go home to his beautiful wife. Instead, Uriah remained at the king's gate for two days, refusing to partake of the pleasures of his bride while his men fought. David then sent Uriah back to the battle with a note to Joab, the leader of the army, requesting that Uriah be put in the front of the line. Uriah was killed and David responded to the news of this valiant soldier's death by telling Joab, "Let not this thing displease thee, for the sword devoureth one as well as another" (2 Sam 11:25). Bathsheba mourned her husband's death, and David took her as his wife (2 Sam 11:26-27).

Equally as important as the events of David's encounter with Bathsheba is the account of Nathan's confrontation of David (2 Sam 12:1-14). It is David's response to Nathan's parable that prevents us from seeing the incidents in 2 Sam 11 as a beautiful story of misguided love. Nathan's words cut through David's heart to reveal the true sin of the matter. Years later, the prophet's conversation with Bathsheba and the crowning of Solomon provide the final sequence in the life of David and Bathsheba (1 Kgs 1).

LIFE IN HER WORLD

When David called for Bathsheba to be brought to his home, she was not confronted by a young shepherd who just happened to have made it to the throne. David's prowess in war (1 Sam 18:7), the anointing early in his life by the prophet Samuel (1 Sam 16:13), and his loyalty to his troops and God made him an extremely popular and powerful king. What happened to Bathsheba in 2 Sam 11 is obvious to some and ambiguous to others. Some theologians and preachers have found fault with Bathsheba and characterized her as everything from the aggressor to the opportunist whose aim in taking the bath was to be placed in a position to become queen and secure the throne for a future son. An examination of Bathsheba's world cannot answer all of the questions of what happened in the palace on that fateful day or for the years after; but, it can give perspective to Bathsheba's situation.

A Normal Life

There are those who suppose that Bathsheba was in an area where she could easily be seen and, therefore, was the seducer of the king. She was not. Houses of the period often had courtyards in the center of the complex.[1] The courtyard would have been secluded from passersby. Bathsheba was bathing inside her home. David's vantage point from his roof plus the benefit of evening shade hid him from her view.

We know that Bathsheba's husband was away at war. Bathsheba was familiar with and surrounded by war. As a military wife, Bathsheba knew David should have been with his men at the front of the Ammonite conflict. After all, it was spring, and the war with the Ammonites had been raging for a year.[2] Bathsheba's husband was already at the front.

Although "most of the account of David's reign was written to glorify David," it seems that Bathsheba had no reason to fear the king or to think that his summons was intended for sexual aggression.[3] David was a musician whose music had soothed King Saul and whose psalms were praises to God (1 Sam 16:18). He was a leader who had always been good to his soldiers and stayed with them through the thick of battle (1 Sam 21). Despite his ability in battle, David was not a violent man. After all he refused to kill King Saul despite the king's efforts to kill him (1 Sam 21). It was David who united all of the tribes of Judah and returned the Ark of the Lord from captivity (2 Sam 5 and 6). Bathsheba had no reason to fear David and, noting Nathan's confrontation with David in 2 Sam 12, neither did anyone else.

Seduction, Rape or Adultery

If we take the position that 2 Sam 11 is a love story, then it is possible to view it as a seductive passage where Bathsheba is lured by the power and prestige of the king. After all, we have no idea if the encounter occurred only once or over a prolonged period of time. We also have no knowledge of Bathsheba's attitude toward the king before, during or after the incident. The matter is further complicated by the fact that Bathsheba, like any woman of her era, had no recourse in the male dominant society.

A more feminist view might consider this passage an account of sexual harassment, sexual assault, and rape —all reprehensible crimes against women. While we categorize rape as a forced sexual violation punishable as a criminal offense, theologian Rebecca Harris points out in an article in the *Pax Pneuma Journal* that "there is no category for sexual assault in Biblical law."[4] Because Hebrew words have several meanings in English, the biblical record is both unclear and unsettling. For example, the New Living Translation (NLT) interprets the words *anah* and *shakab* as "rape" thirteen times. In Gen 34:2, *anah* identifies the "rape" of Jacob's daughter, Dinah. Commentary in *The Jewish Study Bible* also characterizes the assault as rape.[5] In Judg 20:6, the NLT maintains that *anah* describes the rape of a Levite's concubine. *The Jewish Study Bible* and the NLT purport that 2 Sam 13 describes the rape of David's daughter Tamar by his son Amnon.[6] In Gen. 39:14, the NLT translates *shakab* as rape in the false charge of Potiphar's wife against Joseph. Despite the interpretations of the terms, the Mosaic Law regarding rape is narrow and victimizes the woman. Both the NLT and *The Jewish Study Bible* allege rape (*shakab*) in Deuteronomy 22:25-27, the case of a young woman who is assaulted outside of town where her screams cannot be heard. In that case, the woman is not accused of a sin. This loophole would not apply to Bathsheba simply because she was not outside the town but in the king's palace.

The Hebrew Law allows the charge of adultery in Bathsheba's case and counts her guilty of committing sin. Deut 22:22 states, "If a man be found lying with a woman married to an husband, then they shall both of them die, both the man that lay with the woman, and the woman: so shalt thou put away evil from Israel." On the surface, this appears to be Bathsheba's situation and her fate seems sealed with David's. However, even after David is confronted by Nathan, he is neither put to death nor made to atone for his sin. David is exonerated; but, even today, Bathsheba is equated with error.

Family Pain

Regardless of our interpretation of Bathsheba's situation, Rebecca Harris' assertion of rape opens another dialogue:

> The horror of such an experience is unparalleled, and its devastation is far-reaching, wounding more than the ravaged victim. Is there anyone who hurts more for the victim of rape than the victim herself? Yes. It is the man who loves her.[7]

The three men who loved Bathsheba included her husband, Uriah; her father, Eliam; and her grandfather, Ahithophel. After Uriah's death, we hear no more about Eliam, who was also a soldier. He was likely killed in battle. In this scenario, Bathsheba's grandfather experienced grief as great as Bathsheba's. When the spiraling events that led to these deaths are considered, it is evident that Ahithophel felt betrayed by David's actions. When David's son Absalom attempted to take the kingdom from his father, Ahithophel, despite his close association with David, became a confidante to Absalom. Ironically, he vowed to be as loyal to the younger man as he was to his father. When David received this news, he prayed that Ahithophel's advice would be foolish. His prayer worked. The plan was foolish because Ahithophel's aim was not to help Absalom but to degrade David and his household. He suggested that Absalom sleep with his father's concubines.

And all Israel shall hear that thou art abhorred of thy father: then shall the hands of all that are with thee be strong. So they spread Absalom a tent upon the top of the house; and Absalom went in unto his father's concubines in the sight of all Israel" (2 Sam 16: 21-22).

The New Living Translation renders a portion of 2 Sam 16:21 as, "All Israel will know that you have insulted your father beyond hope of reconciliation."

Determined to avenge the honor of his family, Ahithophel's next suggestion was to take soldiers and invade David's camp. When this idea was not accepted,

Ahithophel killed himself (2 Sam 17:23). In the end, Bathsheba is left alone to deal with the loss of her husband, her child, her father, and her grandfather.

GOD IN HER LIFE

Despite her centrality to the events in 2 Sam 11 and 12, Bathsheba is positioned in the background. The biblical account is about David's sin, so her life becomes secondary. For that reason, Bathsheba is not shown in prayer or engaged in an encounter with any angelic being. She is, however, shown to be a woman who observed the law of Moses.

A Household of Faith

When she is seen on the rooftop by David, Bathsheba is not just taking a daily bath. "She had just completed the purification rites after having her menstrual period" (2 Sam 11:4 NLT). Leviticus 15:19-24 states that a woman's menstrual cycle was a source of uncleanness. As a result, the woman remained unclean until the evening of the purification. Bathsheba took a ritual bath that was ceremonially required (Lev 15:19, 26). Obviously, Bathsheba was faithful to her husband, obedient to the Law, and not pregnant when David took her.

Uriah was not an Israelite; he was Hittite. According to the report of the spies Moses sent into the Promised Land, the Hittites were among those tribes that dwelt in the mountains of Canaan (Numbers 13:29). Despite warnings to the contrary, "Hebrews had not only adopted some portion of the Hittites' religious cult soon after the invasion of Palestine, but had intermarried with them."[8] This is exactly what happened with Bathsheba. Uriah, however, seems to have assimilated into the Hebrew culture quite well. He was considered one of the "Thirty Mighty Men" of David's army. He also had, at the very least, reverence for the God of Israel. When David called Uriah home, Uriah's refusal to go to his own house shows his loyalty to the king and the Lord: "The Ark and the armies of Israel and Judah are living in tents, and Joab and my master's men are camping in the open fields. How could I go home to wine and dine and sleep with my wife? I swear that I would never do such a thing" (2 Sam 11:11 NLT).

Her Cries and Obedience

Once we learn that Bathsheba is pregnant, we hear no more from her until Uriah's death. Unlike David, who glibly told Joab not to worry about Uriah's murder, Bathsheba mourned her husband (2 Sam 11:26-27). In the tradition of Israel, the mourning period could have lasted for one week or 30 days. During that time, Bathsheba would have worn mourning clothes. Hebrew custom implies that she would have also torn her clothing, lamented aloud, and made other gestures to indicate her grief.

Bathsheba may also have been lamenting her own fate. She was widowed and pregnant by David and not her husband. In some cases, such as Deut 22:29, the Law provided an option that seems difficult for the modern reader to understand. "For a woman in the ancient near east, there was no hope of restoration. She was permanently ruined—defiled. Her only option was to marry the man who raped her."[9] When Bathsheba's mourning period was over, David came for her and made her his wife. She was obedient to the king and the Law.

Bathsheba was also obedient to the prophet as God's representative. She recognized God's voice when she heeded the advice of the prophet Nathan. In 1 Kgs 11, David was described as old and ill. He had not summoned Nathan or any of his advisors regarding succession after his death. In the meanwhile, David's son Adonijah was preparing to overthrow the throne, but David was unaware of what was happening around him. Nathan went to Bathsheba, knowing the prophecy for the next king, and advised her how to approach David. Through Bathsheba's adherence to the word of the prophet, the coup set forth by Adonijah was spoiled, and Solomon was placed on the throne. Thus, the divine plan for the destiny of Israel was accomplished.

WHAT HER LIFE SPEAKS

Some people have determined that David did not rape Bathsheba because she did not scream. The Bible does not record her voice, and the event is omitted from the book of Chronicles, which generally provides a re-telling of the accounts of the kings. The truth is that because we don't know whether Bathsheba screamed, we don't know how to classify the incident. Except for her cries at the death of her husband (2 Sam 11:27), Bathsheba's voice is silent. We hear no cry when she is summoned to the king's chamber and bedded there. Her voice is silent even in the death of her first born child (2 Sam 12:18). It is years later, near the time of David's death, that we finally hear Bathsheba speak.

There may be reasons the Bible has quieted Bathsheba. We realize that the male-oriented text regarding the Bathsheba encounter centers on the deeds of the king, making her a secondary figure. But, because we have other examples of women's voices when events as horrific as Bathsheba's occur, we know that not all women are silent in the Bible. Nevertheless, Bathsheba's silence has caused us to overlook the spiritual encouragement her life provides.

Concept 1: We Can Decide Our Response to Tragedy
While we may suffer in life, the pain is not ours alone. There are those around us who suffer also. The generational pain that estrangement, shame, and death may have brought upon Bathsheba cannot be known. During her ordeal, Bathsheba lost her husband, her baby, and probably her father. She was also estranged from her grandfather as she left the family home for David's house. At the same time, her grandfather, Ahithophel, lost his son, his granddaughter, and his great-grandchild. Through all of this, Ahithophel was apparently still summoned to the king's side for advice. We cannot know how often Bathsheba and Ahithophel saw one another in David's house or what words were exchanged between them. We do know the pain they suffered had a different effect on each of them.

When Absalom acted to take the crown from his father, it was Ahithophel, Bathsheba's grandfather, who turned away from David to become an advisor to Absalom (2 Sam 15-17). The disgrace Ahithophel desired for David's house is evidenced by the older man's suggestion that Absalom have sex publicly with the concubines and later attack David (2 Sam 16:21; 17:1-3). These suggestions parallel the disgrace David brought on Bathsheba's family.

While Ahithophel sought retaliation and revenge, Bathsheba carried her pain and sorrow in silence. The Bible does not specify her actions, but we know that she was a mother in Israel. The responsibility for rearing children and putting a religious and cultural compass in their early years fell to mothers. Bathsheba did not plot revenge against David. She prepared her son to walk in the path God had ordained for him as King over all Israel and Judah. Ahithophel and Bathsheba faced the same tragedy. Ahithophel's response led to more pain and eventually death. Bathsheba's response gained the favor of God and fulfilled the destiny of the nation.

Concept 2: We Have a Voice

Bathsheba was victimized in many ways, but over time, God gave her a voice. She may have been unheard before; but, when the time came she was able to go to David and he listened to her. Bathsheba's words were clear, and her message was powerful as she pled for her life and the life of her son. Nathan empowered Bathsheba to confront the issues and reminded her that she was the queen. The prophet encouraged her to step into her rightful place as the woman the king loved, the woman who had been at the root of his pleas to God for forgiveness. Bathsheba may have forgotten that God had given her a voice, but God never forgot. At the appointed time, Bathsheba spoke.

When Bathsheba spoke, it was time for the promise to come to pass. It was time for her hope to be realized. It was time for her son to receive the inheritance that was his. It was time for David's throne to be restored according to God's plan. It was time for David to realize that he was still on the throne and had the power to release what God had told him belonged to his son Solomon. It was time to begin the events that would lead to the building of the Temple of God. It was time for Bathsheba and her offspring to walk into the promise of the Lord. It was time for Bathsheba to speak.

Bathsheba's life tells us that we, too, have a voice. One step toward restoration is to prepare spiritually to overcome the issues that silence us. This requires spiritual discipline—prayer, Bible reading, and encouraging ourselves spiritually when the whispers of the past nag us (Eph 5:19; Col 3:16). We must hold tightly to the promises in God's Word. We must "pray through" to release the pain and triumphantly face each day. We have a voice and we have power when we rely upon the Holy Spirit to guide us in seeking spiritual and natural advice and help. This is critical to our Christian journey. We must seek godly and God-directed advice and wisdom, just as Bathsheba heard the instructions of Nathan, whether from the pastor, a spiritual mentor, a family member who puts God first, or a spiritually mature friend. These actions strengthen us so that when the summons to speak is made, we can speak from the place of God's promises rather than our pain. When we are spiritually strong, those around us will not see us as victims anymore, and we will know that our lives have been victorious after all.

Concept 3: We Have the Promise of Life

By the time Bathsheba spoke, David was an old and dying man whose son Adonijah was aggressively taking the kingdom from his father's hand. Instructed by the prophet

Nathan, Bathsheba confronted the king and pled for her life and the life of their son Solomon. She implored David to crown Solomon as promised. The basis of her request was protection and provision for her son, the nation, and herself. She explained the gravity of the situation. "...It shall come to pass, when my lord the king shall sleep with his fathers, that I and my son Solomon shall be counted offenders" (1 Kgs 1:21). Bathsheba had every reason to believe that upon David's death, she and Solomon would be killed. However, because she did not concede defeat, her life speaks hope to us today.

Bathsheba held on to the promise she had been given. In 1 Kgs 1:17, she said to David, "My lord, thou swarest by the LORD thy God unto thine handmaid, saying, 'Assuredly Solomon thy son shall reign after me, and he shall sit upon my throne.'" She had held on to that promise since the death of her first child. Her hope was that King David would act to honor his chosen son. Her concern was not selfish. Bathsheba realized that crowning Solomon would also secure the nation. In her boldness, she declared, "And thou, my lord, O king, the eyes of all Israel are upon thee, that thou shouldest tell them who shall sit on the throne of my lord the king after him" (1 Kgs 1:20).

Bathsheba's life says that despite the losses we suffer and the pain we bear, God never leaves us alone. While others may try to silence us or, even worse, ignore what we have been through and our pleas for help, God has not forgotten. No matter how things unfold and how little concern others have for our well-being, God has not forsaken us. We can still expect the promises of God to come true. They may not come when we expect them or in the manner we imagine, but what God has promised will come to pass.

Because of the sacrifice of Jesus Christ, Christians can seek God's mercy, grace, healing, and forgiveness. Focusing on the Word of God and the sacrifice Jesus Christ made on our behalf gives Christians the courage to let go of overpowering feelings of despair. There is no evidence that Bathsheba did anything wrong, yet the pain of her suffering can be felt. The interpretation of her violation has often unfairly attributed shame to her. Perhaps pain and shame led her grandfather to plot revenge on David's house, to destroy the reputation of David's son, and to eventually take his own life. But Bathsheba walked in the promise and not the past. Because of Jesus, we can, too.

Bathsheba's life speaks to all Christians, but it offers special comfort to women who have suffered sexual harassment, rape, and widowhood. She speaks to those women who have lost their children to death from horrific illness. Her life speaks to all who have had their lives altered by violence. Bathsheba's life touches each of our lives even if our situations are vastly different from hers. Her life teaches us that while tribulation occurs in the lives of Christians and non-Christians alike, the difference must be in the way we handle that pain. No one can undo an injustice or escape the trepidation of living. However, as Christians, we have promises of God that are sure (2 Cor 1:20; 2 Peter 1:4). When we hold those promises before us, we can claim them as our own. Even when the possibility seems dim, we can train our focus on things above (Col 3:2) knowing that the promises of God are true.

Hearing Bathsheba

WHAT YOUR LIFE SPEAKS

Speak Your Truth
1. Is there a pain, problem, person, or situation that has silenced you? If so, describe it.
2. How have you responded to your silencing in the past?
3. What is your first step in changing or confronting the silence?

Focus Your Faith
1. Scriptures throughout the Bible identify the promises of God. Select several promises and identify the specific assurance each gives you. How can you incorporate these promises into your daily devotion?
2. Who have you talked to or should talk to for spiritual advice, direction, or encouragement? What other support (medical, psychological, social, legal) will help you address the issue that has silenced you?

USING YOUR VOICE

Ponder
1. How has examining Bathsheba's social and cultural history helped you connect with her life?
2. What resources and help do you need to begin a personal Bible study or devotion?

Pray
1. Ask God to give you a greater sensitivity to people

who are facing abuse, harassment, bullying, and other social silencers.

2. Seek God's healing for the physical, emotional, and spiritual wounds you or others have experienced through abuse or mistreatment.

Practice

1. Volunteer at a shelter, call center, hospital, or other facility that helps people who have suffered from abuse.

2. Identify agencies in your area where you can turn for help or refer others who seek help from domestic violence or healing from sadness or grief.

Leah

GENESIS 29-33

HAVE YOU EVER WONDERED WHY there are so many love songs? Pop, jazz, classical, blues, country, R & B, even hip-hop, celebrate love found and lament love lost. Good love, bad love, forbidden love, misguided love—all are fair game for a song. The reason is simple: Love is a universal emotion. So why doesn't "love" have the last say? Because, whether we like it or not, love is governed by societal norms.

Our culture determines the answer to questions such as: Who can I marry? When am I old enough or experienced enough for a commitment? What is the "acceptable" solution when I can't be with the one I love? How do I know when love and marriage are successful? How can I respond when love disappoints me? Our American ideas of love and marriage, family and success don't seem remotely related to those concepts in Old Testament times. For example, how can we relate our concept of courtship to the arranged marriage that Jacob's first wife, Leah, experienced? In order to have empathy for Leah's understanding of the marital relationship, we must transport our hearts and minds to an earlier era. Only then can we recognize that her longing for a successful relationship is not far from our desire today. But, to understand the frustration she faced we have to walk in her shoes.

SYNOPSIS

Leah lived in Haran with her father, Laban, her younger sister, Rachel, and her brothers (Gen 31:1). Since the text makes no mention of a mother, we must assume that the mother has died. Thus, Leah probably took care of the home while Rachel tended the flocks of sheep the family raised. In Gen 29, Jacob arrived in Haran where he met Rachel at the well where she watered the sheep. He explained that he was a relative. His mother, Rebekah, was Rachel's father's sister. When Rachel took back news of this newly arrived nephew, Laban came to and take Jacob home.

Once there, Jacob met Leah, Rachel's older sister. After he had explained how he came to be at his uncle's house, Jacob was accepted as a relative and worked on his uncle's land. At the end of the month, Laban said it was unfair for him to work Jacob without wages. He asked the young man what he desired for pay. Jacob replied, "I will serve thee seven years for Rachel thy younger daughter."

Laban agreed, and Jacob continued to work (Gen 29:18-19).

At the end of the seven years, Jacob asked that he be given his bride (Gen 29:21). Laban made a feast to celebrate the wedding and gave his daughter a handmaid as a wedding gift. As the evening progressed, however, Laban took Leah to the bridal chamber instead of Rachel. It was not until the next morning—after the marriage had been consummated—that Jacob saw what had been done. Jacob's loud protests were met by Laban's calm response. The elder man blamed the misunderstanding on tradition. His explanation was simple: "In our country" the elder sister must marry before the younger.

To rectify the situation, Laban decided that when the weeklong bridal feast ended, Rachel would be given to Jacob. She, too, would have a handmaid. However, if Jacob wanted Rachel, he had to pay a price: seven more years in his uncle's service. He had worked for one bride. Leah might have been the wrong bride, but a bride she was. For fourteen years of labor, Jacob would get two handmaids and two brides, one of which was the woman he loved. The deal was struck; the deed was done.

The following week, Rachel became the second bride and was transferred to her husband without fanfare or pomp. The Bible does not say how Rachel felt about the situation; but, any dreams the younger sister had of what life would be like after the seven years of service were dashed.

We do know how Leah felt. She was distraught and lamented that her husband did not love her. As a result, she was in competition with her sister for Jacob's affection.

Because Rachel was barren, Leah used childbirth as leverage in her fight to win Jacob's love. She gave birth to four sons: Reuben, Simeon, Levi, and Judah (Gen 29:32-35).

Rachel resorted to surrogate adoption through her handmaid, Bilhah (Gen 30:3). Through this servant, Rachel essentially adopted two sons for Jacob: Dan and Naphtali (Gen 30: 6 and 8). As if in retaliation, Leah gave Jacob her handmaid, Zilpah who birthed Gad and Asher (Gen 30:10-13). Leah later gave birth to two more sons, Issachar and Zebulun, and a daughter, Dinah (Gen 30: 17-21). Finally, Rachel bore a son, Joseph (Gen 30:23-24); but, she later died in childbirth with her second son, Benjamin (Gen 35:18).

In Gen 31, Jacob and his family took all they had and fled Laban's house. Chapters 32 through 35 of Genesis record the journey. In Gen 35:9-10, Jacob had an encounter with God, who "blessed him and ... said unto him, Thy name is Jacob: thy name shall not be called any more Jacob, but Israel shall be thy name: and he called his name Israel." When the journey was complete, Leah and her husband had returned to the land of his father with the sons who would be called the Twelve Tribes of Israel.

LIFE IN HER WORLD

Leah lived in the rural area of Haran. Through her we view a specific household and learn its connection to the patriarchs of Israel. In many ways, Leah's life is typical of her era. Through her we hear the cries of an ordinary woman in her quest for love and value.

Marriage Customs

Marriage among the patriarchs was monogamous, which

was in contrast to pagan cultures where polygamy was the norm. Typical marriages of this period were arranged by the fathers of the couple, often without the couple having ever met. It was preferable to marry within the clan (endogamy) in order to continue the traditions and customs of the tribe. For ancient cultures, marriage began with a betrothal. A betrothal was a binding contract that included a payment from the groom to the bride's family since she would no longer contribute to the family economy. This was known as a bride price. Although the marriage would not be consummated until much later, a woman who was betrothed was considered to be a legally married person.[1] The actual wedding ceremony was a time of celebration. Families were expected to give a gift to the bride. The community was invited to the wedding feast, which lasted for seven days. This celebration was considered the bride week. During the wedding ceremony, the veiled bride was taken to the bridal chamber secretly, and the groom was escorted there later by friends.[2]

Jacob's request to marry Rachel was arranged with a bride price of seven years of labor. Jacob was faithful in fulfilling his obligation, and Laban provided all of the symbols of an official wedding. He set a wedding feast and invited the community. He gave his daughter a handmaid as her gift. It is only in his substitution of Leah for Rachel that we see Laban's disregard for tradition and culture. He had, however, laid the foundation for his actions long before the wedding day.

The agreement between Laban and Jacob regarding the marriage had been very informal (Gen 29). There was no mention of an outside witness or an official betrothal ceremony. Without these formalities, Laban was free to view the arrangement as a non-binding promise rather than a legal betrothal. Thus switching the brides became Laban's prerogative. Jacob, however, understood the arrangement to be binding. He was right to be outraged at Laban's deception. Furthermore, Jacob was marrying within the clan and fully expected to have only one bride. In essence, Laban forced Jacob into a polygamous arrangement.

While the biblical emphasis is on Jacob's anger, Leah was upset as well. Despite the fact that she was a substitute bride, Laban's promise that Jacob could have Rachel at the end of Leah's bride week marred Leah's wedding. It also cheated Rachel out of the marriage she was promised. Laban's disdain for marriage and tradition was displayed in full view of the neighbors who had gathered for the celebration. The deception was public, and Leah bore the brunt of the disregard and shame.

In Her Father's House

In some rabbinical literature, Laban's name is said to mean "glowing with wickedness."[3] While this is not the literal translation of his name, it seems appropriate in light of Laban's actions in the Genesis record. Jacob's explanation of how he came to stay with his uncle included telling "all things." Rather than being sympathetic to his nephew's plight, Laban saw an opportunity to take advantage of Jacob, marry off both his daughters, and get free labor as well.

Laban had at least two reasons for his actions. First, Laban may have felt he would not find another prospect for his older daughter. Interpretations have portrayed Leah as an unattractive young woman who wasn't marriage material. While those characterizations are likely exaggerated, Laban's actions demonstrated his disregard of Leah. If Laban's later assertion about the custom of marrying the older daughter first is to be believed, his failure to state that during negotiations was a slap in Leah's face as she realized she was being overlooked. The conversation between Laban and Jacob signaled that Leah was neither pretty enough to be wanted nor valuable enough to be offered. Second, Laban remembered the display of wealth in Jacob's family. Jacob's grandfather, Abraham, sent ten camels bearing gifts when he took Laban's sister, Rebekah, as a bride for Jacob's father, Isaac (Gen 24). Laban's memory of that display of wealth coupled with his greed, seem likely motives to take advantage of Jacob.

The sisters knew their father and his capacity for treachery. When Jacob proposed leaving Laban, the sisters replied, "That's fine with us! We won't inherit any of our father's wealth anyway. He has reduced our rights to those of foreign women. And after he sold us, he wasted the money you paid him for us. All the wealth God has given you from our father legally belongs to us and our children. So go ahead and do whatever God has told you" (Gen 31:14-16 NLT).

Contention and deception were generational traits in Laban's family. Both Laban and his sister are depicted as the instigators of the conflict among their children. Jacob was one of the twin sons of Laban's sister. He and his twin brother, Esau, fought in their mother's womb (Gen 25:22). Although Jacob was the younger brother, he was more cunning than Esau. He managed to swindle his famished brother out of his birthright with the promise of food (v. 33). It was their mother who conceived of Jacob's plot to steal Esau's blessing from their ill and feeble father. When the deception was discovered, she feared that Esau would kill his brother so she convinced their father to send Jacob to Haran to stay with her brother Laban to escape the wrath of Esau (Gen 27). Jacob and Esau finally resolved their issues (Gen 32), but they had spent most of their years estranged.

The relationship between Leah and Rachel grew more contentious during the marriages. Leah was the older daughter, but Rachel was the favored one (Gen 29:17). The events put in place by Laban compounded Leah's despair. Her rejection was compounded when he substituted her in the bridal bed and then offered a "package deal" on her wedding day. The married life that began with Leah's bridal week was marred by her husband's rejection, her public disgrace by her father, and the encroachment on her home by her sister. Leah seemed destined for a life of disappointment and shame.

The Importance of Children

In ancient Israel, "childbearing conferred prestige and position on a woman because of the advantage of numerous children to the economic livelihood of her family... (childbirth was a way to) perpetuate the lineage of her husband."[4] Women were expected to produce children. Not being able to give birth was considered a curse and showed God's displeasure. If they could not bear children themselves, then barren women had to find another way to remove the sting of this failure.

Israel often followed the cultural codes of other societies. According to the Sumerian Laws of Ur-Nammu, a wife could give a slave, a servant, or a concubine to the husband so that a child could be produced.[5] The use of concubines as surrogates and secondary wives was accepted without question across ancient people groups.[6] The process of birthing children through this surrogacy was known as having a child "on the knees of the wife." It was a type of adoption although the surrogate was often identified as the birth mother (Gen 30:3). The children were co-heirs with any other children born to that father. It was customary for the wife to suggest the use of the concubine as a secondary wife. It was fully acceptable then for Leah and Rachel to give their handmaids to Jacob. The children born to Jacob by the handmaids were considered the children of Leah and Rachel.

Sister Against Sister: The Birthing Race

Jacob chose Rachel, but Leah was his first wife. Jacob's choice (and subsequently, Laban's actions) positioned Leah and Rachel as rivals for Jacob's love from the beginning of the marriages. Leah realized that she could not win Jacob's heart with her looks and feminine wiles, but because God's hand was on her, she hoped to win him through childbearing.

In Gen 30 the sisters clash through an incident over mandrakes picked by Leah's oldest son, Reuben. This fruit, referred to as "love apples," was thought to be an aphrodisiac with the power to promote fertility.[7] Rachel's request for the fruit led to Leah's outburst: "Is it a small matter that thou hast taken my husband? and wouldest thou take away my son's mandrakes also?" (Gen 30:15) Leah had harbored her frustration since her wedding week indicating that, despite her having given birth to six sons, Rachel still managed to capture Jacob's heart.

The mandrake incident provided an opportunity for Leah to confront Jacob's attitude toward her. Rachel traded a night with Jacob for the mandrakes, but Leah was afraid that Jacob would still go to Rachel's tent. This would mean she would lose her prime (and purchased) opportunity to have one night with him. Leah accosted Jacob as he came out of the field that evening. Her raw frustration and desperation indicated that Jacob possibly had left her bed completely. "Thou *must* come in unto me; for surely I have *hired* thee with my son's mandrakes." Leah shamelessly put everything on the line. It is as if she is saying, "I paid for you, and you are obligated to come to me tonight." Jacob did. While the statement implies that Leah purchased Jacob's favor for only one night, he apparently went back on several occasions. Genesis 30:17-21 says that Leah gave birth to two more sons and a daughter.

GOD IN HER LIFE

While we do not see Leah engaged in religious rituals, we do find indications of the religious nature of her home and her life. Her father was an idolater who worshiped handcrafted gods. When Jacob gathered his wives, children, and livestock to leave Laban's home, Laban followed claiming they had "stolen" his gods (Gen 31:30). It turned out that Rachel, the favored wife, had stolen the icons and hidden them beneath her seat. While Jacob was unaware of the theft at the time he was confronted by Laban, Gen 35:2-4 reveals he was aware of it later.

Then Jacob said unto his household, and to all that were with him, Put away the strange gods that are among you, and be clean, and change your garments: And let us arise, and go up to Bethel; and I will make there an altar unto God, who answered me in the day of my distress, and was with me in the way which I went. And they gave unto Jacob all the strange gods which were in their hand, and all their earrings which were in their ears; and Jacob hid them under the oak which was by Shechem.

There is no indication where Leah stood regarding idols. However, throughout the Genesis account God is attributed with blessing Leah to have children. Genesis 29:31 says that "when the LORD saw that Leah was hated, he opened her womb..." God's actions demonstrated that while Rachel may have had the favor of man, Leah had divine favor. Throughout her marriage, Leah's hope and frustration were displayed in the meanings of the names she gave her children. At first the names arose from her cries for her husband's attention. Later they morphed into pleas for God's mercy, declarations of her resolve, and pronouncements of God's deliverance. The names of Leah's children reveal her faith journey.

Reuben – This name meant "See! A son." It was also a plea. In Gen 29:32, Leah gave voice to her frustration. With the birth of Reuben, Leah said that God had *seen* for Himself that she was hated. "Surely the LORD hath looked upon my affliction; now therefore my husband will love me." Leah was grateful for what God had done and believed the birth would garner her husband's attention.

Simeon – His name meant "hearing." Leah no longer suffered in silence. Instead, she cried out to the Lord in prayer. Through Simeon's name, Leah declared that "Because the LORD hath heard I was hated, he hath therefore given me this son" (Gen 29:33).

Levi – This third son's name meant "attached." Leah desperately prayed to be attached to her husband. She was obviously looking for something beyond conjugal duty. By now Jacob should have seen her value as a wife and mother. Her only desire was to be bound to Jacob. She cried that there had been no intimate intertwining of their lives.

Judah – The birth of son four marked a difference in Leah's perspective. In naming him, Leah praised God. She was weary of crying and expecting her husband to respond. Instead, she displayed her resolve. She was a faithful mother and dutiful wife. She would no longer see herself as a victim. Instead, she would praise God for what He had done and declare herself victorious.

After the birth of Judah, Leah "left bearing" and believed she could not have any more children, but Leah's peace was short-lived. She became the adoptive mother of the children born to Jacob by her handmaid Zilpah and named those children as well.

Gad – The King James Version of the Bible says that Gad, the name of the first child born through Zilpah, means "a troop cometh." Theologians seem to agree, however, that a better translation is "good fortune" or "lucky." The New Living Translation, as well as the *Orthodox Jewish Bible*, render Gad's name as "How fortunate I am!" (Gen 30:11).

Asher – When Zilpah gave birth to a second son, Leah named him Asher, which means "happy." The New Living Translation renders this, "What joy is mine! Now the other women will celebrate with me" (Gen 30:13).

Following the mandrake payoff, Jacob returned to Leah's bed, and she gave birth to three more children.

Issachar – This son's name was the Hebrew *sakhar*. It is translated as "wages or salary." Through this name, Leah declared that "God has rewarded me for giving my servant to my husband as a wife" (Gen 30:18 NLT). The translation of this Old Testament passage by Robert Alter in *The Five Books of Moses* compares the use of the word *sakhar*, which means "a fee paid," to Leah's use of this same word when she demanded that Jacob come to her tent because of the fee in mandrakes that she paid to Rachel.[8]

Zebulun – This final son's name meant "He will bring an award." Through him she declares, "God has given me a good reward. Now my husband will treat me with respect, for I have given him six sons" (Gen 30:20 NLT).

Dinah – Finally, Leah bore a daughter for Jacob. There was no naming ceremony for girls, but Leah named her

Dinah, which meant "justice." Leah had endured. She had finally gotten justice through the birth of her children.

WHAT HER LIFE SPEAKS

Leah's life speaks to us about determination and faith. Leah keeps the faith no matter what befalls her. She was rejected by her father and treated as a lesser child despite the fact she was "the first born" (Gen 29:26). She was essentially cheated out of the honor due her as Jacob's first wife, but she maintained her faith that God would vindicate her. For today's Christians, Leah's life is a practical example of our struggle to recognize and embrace God's will in all things. While her first three sons' names focused on what she wanted to happen, the names of the last six children emphasized what God was doing and had done in her life. Through their names, we observe Leah's development into a woman who was determined to persevere despite the disappointments she faced.

Concept 1: God Knows and Understands our Distress (Reuben, Simeon, and Levi)

Leah was raised by a father who discounted her. She ended up with a husband who rejected her. She lived in lifelong conflict with her sister. Traditionally, she would have left Laban's house to go to Jacob's father's house when she and Jacob married. Because Laban added seven more years to Jacob's servitude, her marriage became a trap that kept her at her father's home. Unable to escape the turmoil that characterized her life, Leah concentrated on her frustration. Through her actions, Leah declared to the world that she was unloved.

We see people in Leah's plight every day. Think about the people you know who feel they must work to gain the acceptance of others. Consider the people who think that if they don't pay the entire lunch bill or provide the ride for the evening, their friends will not spend time with them. Age is not a factor in this thinking. In a recent case, one senior citizen reported to her pastor that people were stealing from her. When the pastor investigated the situation, he discovered that she constantly gave money away—even to store clerks—because she felt they deserved something for being nice to her.

Leah's desperation for a relationship that valued and appreciated her is no different from a woman's desire for those things today. Like Leah, some women, whether they are married or sexually active without marriage, believe that their sexual favors, or even having a baby, will help them keep the man. Too often, women discover that, like Leah, their effort achieves only more anxiety. Leah used her children's names to vent her frustration. Today, women may wear a facade to hide their real feelings from friends and family—but God knows the hidden things, the secret things in our hearts. When we view the names of Leah's first three sons, we realize that God sees our predicaments. God hears our prayers and knows our innermost desires. God recognizes our longing for genuine relationships that honor who we are and value us for it.

Concept 2: We Must Praise God Through It All (Judah)

While her sister was the shepherd who worked outside the house, the absence of a mother meant that Leah was the one who took care of the house. She accepted that role and continued to serve in that capacity after marriage. By the time Leah gave birth to Judah, she had realized her husband still did not see her merit. She had been successful in reaching the goal for women of her day. Society expected her to fulfill her duties as a wife and to provide children, especially sons, for her husband. She did that. With the birth of Judah, Leah said, "Now I will praise the Lord." In every way possible for a young woman of her time, Leah had been successful—but it took her four sons to realize it.

Sometimes we, too, forget the daily triumphs we experience and fail to see the good things that happen in our lives. These daily markers of grace may not look or feel like we thought they would, but they are meritorious in their own way. An old gospel chorus tells us to count our blessings. When we fail to count the blessings of each day, we run the risk of being overtaken by negativity. When we look outside our own successes and find our dreams in what others are doing, we show disdain for the blessings in our lives. Before we know it, we seek our own will rather than God's will for us.

No matter the circumstance, Judah's name says that we must praise God. Despite any setbacks, we must praise the Lord knowing that Jesus Christ is the "author and finisher of our faith" (Hebrews 12:2). We all have had expectations for our lives that didn't happen as we imagined. In our self-pity, we forget that God knew what would happen. We fail to remember that God also knew the outcome of it all. When our plans for "the good life" don't reach the levels we expect, like Leah, we must shift our line of sight. If we continue to focus on what we don't have and what didn't happen, we will forget to see the blessings before us.

Leah's life teaches us that when we praise the Lord for what He has provided, we find contentment that is beyond measure and joy that is satisfying to our souls. When we begin to praise God rather than focusing on our chief complaints, we can "leave bearing." We can be free from the process of trying to birth our own ideas and outcomes. We can leave the pain of seeing ourselves through what we imagine we should be. We can stop trying to live up to the expectations of others. We can stop carrying the burden of not measuring up to an arbitrary standard or even our own expectations of perfection. When we praise God despite the pain, despair and doubt, we can move to a place of joy in the Lord.

Concept 3: God's Grace Suffices (Gad, Asher, Issachar, Zebulun, and Dinah)

Some Christians don't accept the concept of "luck," but we can look at Gad's name as the abundance of grace from God. When we realize what the Lord has provided for us and where He has taken us, we realize that we are more than fortunate. We are "blessed and highly favored!" The happiness Leah identified through the birth of Asher reminds Christians to be happy in Christ Jesus. An old Pentecostal chorus says, "This joy that I have, the world didn't give it to me. And if the world didn't give it, the world can't take it away!" The joy of the Lord helps us recognize the grace God has given us despite the problems we face.

In naming Issachar, Zebulun, and Dinah, Leah proclaims three principles of grace:

1. Jesus paid it all – Issachar's name meant "wages." In his name, we are reminded that "The wages of sin is death;

but the gift of God is eternal life through Jesus Christ our Lord" (Rom 6:23). The price for sin is no longer our debt. Instead, we reap the benefit of all Jesus did on Calvary. The chorus to a timeless hymn proclaims,

> *Jesus paid it all.*
> *All to Him I owe.*
> *Sin had left a crimson stain;*
> *He washed it white as snow.* [9]

The sacrifice of Christ makes it possible for us to have hope for tomorrow as well as strength for today. Generally, we think only about the physical healing we have through Christ; but His sacrifice goes much further. As we focus on His grace and mercy in delivering us from our fears and woes, we are healed. Through His sacrifice, our anxiety and trepidation are healed. By His stripes we are delivered from the shame that has too long been the tenor of our lives. The shed blood of Jesus Christ covers not only our wrongs but our hurts. The price has been paid so that we are free to live victoriously.

2. Christ is the reward – Christianity is not a "pie-in-the-sky" religion. Our hope is not in the next life only. We have hope for our days on earth as well. Zebulun's name reminds us that our struggle is over; our vexation is done. It is in Christ that our heads are lifted and our tears wiped away. When we turn to Jesus Christ as Lord and Savior, He makes a difference in our lives. When we accept Christ's gift of salvation, we are awarded by Him with new life. "This means that anyone who belongs to Christ has become a new person. The old life is gone; a new life has begun" (2 Cor 5:17 NLT). This newness signals a change in our thinking and our behavior.

Because the indwelling of the Holy Spirit makes us new creatures, we are reconciled to Christ. We are also given a new mission in life—to reconcile others to Christ (2 Cor 5:18). As His ambassadors, we are empowered by the Holy Spirit to spread the Good News of salvation because we have been delivered and set free. Even more, we are able to recognize that life in this world is not all there is. We have hope for each day and hope in the eternal manifestation of life with Christ.

The award in Christ Jesus is endless. It is neither a pittance nor a payoff. The award of Christ goes far beyond what we "bargained for" and takes us into the heavenly realms. That is why we can pray despite discouragement. His award is the reason we can praise in the face of crisis. In Christ, we have the gift of God's love, which covers everything and redirects our entire world. Our responses change and our associations become new as we walk in the realization that we are ambassadors for Christ (2 Cor 5:20).

3. By grace we are free – "There is therefore now no condemnation to them which are in Christ Jesus, who walk not after the flesh, but after the Spirit" (Rom 8:1). Dinah's name means "justice" and reminds Christians that we are justified in Christ and are righteous before the Lord. When we have been born again our status with God changes. While we were seen as sinners before, we are now vindicated through God's grace. Where we were destined to pay the penalty for sin, we are now redeemed by Christ Jesus before the throne of God's grace. Despite what the years of low self-esteem, hurt, shame, and pain may have done, God's grace lifts our heads to realize we can stand before God through the victory He has given us (Rom 3:25). Indeed, God's grace is sufficient (2 Cor 12:9).

Hear Leah

WHAT YOUR LIFE SPEAKS

Speak Your Truth

1. Leah's life was painful, and she struggled to get beyond it. Is there hurt in your life that you cannot seem to get beyond? How has that hurt been acted out through your life?
2. Leah's life hinged on failed relationships. Is there a relationship in your life that needs healing? How have you sought to rectify or release it?

Focus Your Faith

1. Select one or more of the names Leah gave her children, and look for Scriptures that give insight into that concept. How can you incorporate those Scriptures into your daily devotion?
2. What spiritual support will help you address an issue that has been a struggle in your life?

USING YOUR VOICE

Ponder

1. Leah was able to cry to the Lord because she knew the Lord. How well do you know Him? What is your relationship with Jesus Christ?
2. We can never know the Lord completely. How are you seeking to know Him better each day?

Pray

1. Think about people you know who, like Leah, live in difficult situations. Create a prayer list of those people and pray earnestly for them on a daily basis.

2. Leah cried out to God through the names of her children. How have you asked God to help you?

Practice

1. If you have overcome an issue and are strong enough to talk about it, seek an opportunity to share your testimony with others who are still struggling. You may want to speak with your pastor to determine the best venue for you to do this.

2. Rejection such as Leah suffered can lead to depression and even suicide. Work with a group in your church or community to have a medical professional discuss the symptoms of depression and suicide and to provide suggestions regarding help for those who may be struggling with physical and emotional stress.

DISCUSSION THREE

Esther

THE BOOK OF ESTHER

THE STORY OF CINDERELLA is a captivating account of an orphaned girl who is forced to live with an evil stepmother and jealous stepsisters before being swept away by the handsome prince. At first glance, we might think of Esther's life as a "Cinderella story" come true. NOT! The twists and turns of Esther's journey as an orphaned child who goes from her uncle's house to the king's palace reveals a woman who would be the first to tell us that Cinderella was all in for herself, but Esther was all in for a much larger purpose and plan.

SYNOPSIS

King Ahasuerus (King Xerxes) is first mentioned in Esther 1:1, where a description of court life during the third year of his reign captures the reader's attention.[1] It was during that banquet that King Ahasuerus banished his wife, Queen Vashti, for her refusal to appear before the king and his court. Three years later, in the sixth year of his reign, a search for a new queen was started. The king demanded that virgins from all quarters of his kingdom be brought to Shushan, his summer residence. When the candidates for queen arrived at the palace, they were taken through a yearlong grooming process. When the beautification period was over, each woman spent one night with the king.[2] If the king was pleased, the woman was taken to the quarters of the concubines. They would never go before the king again unless he summoned them.

Among the virgins was a young orphan. Her Hebrew name was Hadassah; her Persian name was Esther. Following the death of her parents, Esther was adopted by her uncle Mordecai. Although she was reared in the Jewish tradition, Mordecai cautioned Esther not to reveal to the king's men that she was a Jew (Esther 2:10, 19). When she arrived in Shushan, her beauty and charm were noted by Hegai, the servant charged with caring for the women. He selected the best servants, chamber, and food for her. Esther's night with the king came in the seventh year of Ahasuerus' reign (Esther 1:3; 2:16). "The king loved Esther above all the women, and she obtained grace and favour in his sight more than all the virgins; so that he set the royal crown upon her head, and made her queen instead of Vashti" (Esther 2:17).

During her yearlong grooming process, Esther's uncle Mordecai passed the king's gate daily to check on his niece's welfare (Esther 2:11). Esther 2:21 implies that Mordecai obtained a position in the palace following Esther's elevation to the throne.[3] It was then that he overheard a plot by two of the king's chamberlains to kill the king. He reported this to Esther, who told the king of the coup and credited Mordecai with having revealed the matter. When the assassination attempt was investigated and found to be true, the would-be assassins were killed.

Soon after these events, the king appointed his servant Haman to be the chief official of the Empire. The elevation required everyone to bow in Haman's presence. Mordecai, however, repeatedly and consistently refused to bow saying, "I am a Jew" (Esther 3:4). The insulted Haman then convinced the king that there was a race of people who were disloyal to the crown and should be destroyed. The king agreed to the annihilation, and Haman went forth with his plan. He even pulled lots, or "pur," to decide the specific date on which all Jews throughout the empire would be killed (vv. 6-14).

From that point, Esther was engaged by Mordecai to find a remedy that would save her people and herself. Convinced of what she must do and the danger she faced, Esther called for a three-day fast. She engaged her palace servants, as well as all of the Jews in Shushan, in this ritual. At the end of the three days, she positioned herself outside the king's window. When he noticed her and extended the scepter, she invited the king and Haman to a banquet. Once there the king asked what favor Esther wished granted. She requested only that the king and Haman come the next night for another feast. At that time, she would make her request of the king.

When Haman left the banquet, he was very pleased; but, he saw Mordecai and became enraged. At home, Haman bragged of all he had and of the honor the queen had given him by inviting him to the banquet. He complained, however, that the very sight of Mordecai spoiled everything. Haman's wife, Zeresh, advised him to have a gallows constructed so that Mordecai could be hanged on it the next day. Haman agreed.

That night, unable to sleep, King Ahasuerus perused the royal archives. He found that no honor had been bestowed upon the man who thwarted the assassination plot. The next day Haman had the gallows built, but before he could petition the king to hang Mordecai, he was summoned to the royal chamber. The king asked Haman what honor the loyal subject should receive. Thinking that he must be the one to be honored, Haman explained the royal gifts and honor due that man. The king then had Haman bestow those honors upon Mordecai. Distraught, Haman followed the king's mandate but went home immediately afterward to mourn. Before he could create a counter-plot, he was called to the queen's second feast.

As they ate, Esther revealed that she was a Jew and requested that her life and the life of her people be saved. When she told the king that Haman was the man who had plotted their deaths, the king became so angry that he left the room and went into the garden. When he returned, he found Haman on Esther's sofa. Haman had fallen into her lap, begging her to help him because he knew the king was going to kill him. King Ahasuerus, however, thought Haman was trying to rape the queen. When the guards came to take Haman, one of the soldiers stated there was a gallows available. In the end, Haman was hanged on the gallows that he built for Mordecai, the Jews were saved, and Esther was endeared in the hearts of Jews worldwide. She is celebrated annually as the heroine of the Jewish festival of Purim. She is also recognized by Christians as the woman who understood and was obedient to God's intent for her life.

LIFE IN HER WORLD

The events in the book of Esther occur 103 years following the destruction of the Temple and the city of Jerusalem by King Nebuchadnezzar of Babylon. The Hebrew inhabitants, including royalty, were led captive to Babylon and given the name "Jews." In 539 B.C., King Cyrus of Persia overthrew Nebuchadnezzar, and the captives became part of the Persian Empire. In 538 B.C., Cyrus allowed the Jewish captives to return to Jerusalem. Some did, and their return is recounted in the books of Ezra and Nehemiah. Other Jews stayed in Persia. Though they remained citizens of the Persian Empire, they retained their Jewish faith. Several Old Testament books, including Daniel, Nehemiah, Ezra, and Esther, detail life in Babylon and Persia.

The book of Esther has proven to be problematic for theologians for several reasons. First, there is no identifiable author. Scholars believe the writer was a Jewish resident of Persia whose family was taken captive in the overthrow of the Babylonian Empire. This is supported by the lack of discussion regarding life in Jerusalem and the extensive information about life in the Persian court. The next argument is that the real purpose of the book of Esther was to give an account of the events that led to the

Jewish festival of Purim since the entire book focuses on the preservation and perseverance of the Jews in Persia. Because the book of Esther is not part of the Jewish Torah, rabbis and Jewish scholars view it as a "comedy" that draws on the tradition of storytelling and exaggeration.[4] Rabbis concede that the book of Esther is critical in promoting the identity and solidarity among Jews of the Diaspora.[5] The greatest criticism, however, is that the book of Esther does not directly mention God. The Christian Bible deems it a sacred text that describes human actions but never discounts God's presence. While scholars might have a problem with the book of Esther, Christians embrace it because "the book is driven by implicit accounts of God's faithfulness and sovereignty, even though His name is unmentioned."[6]

Life in the Persian Court

The book of Esther describes life in the Persian Empire under the reign of King Ahasuerus (King Xerxes). The palace at Shushan was massive and decorated to demonstrate the wealth of the king. The first chapter of Esther provides a vivid description of a great hall with "white, green, and blue hangings fastened with cords of fine linen and purple." These were attached by "silver rings and pillars of marble." The sofas (beds) around the rooms were made of "gold and silver." The floors beneath were paved with "red, and blue, and white, and black, marble" (Esther 1:6).

The Persian Empire included 127 provinces that spanned from "India to Ethiopia." Because of the diversity of people in Persia, all decrees and letters were sent in several languages. Esther 8:10 describes the Persian mail system, which allowed these missives to be sent to all of the provinces "by posts on horseback, and riders on mules, camels, and young dromedaries." The global scope of the empire was also addressed through the king's custom of including the advice of his governors and satraps (Persian provincial princes) in all decisions regarding the kingdom. In fact, the administration of the realm was quite efficient. The Persians were exceptionally good record keepers and archivists. Everything regarding the empire was meticulously recorded and filed in a manner that made retrieval of information manageable.

Two of the official implements of the king's authority were the seal and the golden scepter. The scepter was used to grant or deny permission for anyone, male or female, to come before the king. Approaching the king without his approval was punishable by death (Esther 4:11). The king's seal was likely a signet ring that held a particular inscription. The royal seal was used to transfer the king's emblem onto a document to authenticate it. Decrees made by the king and set with his seal could not be revoked. The book of Daniel describes this in explaining a plot to have Daniel killed by a den of lions (Dan 6:8). When Esther asked King Ahasuerus to reverse Haman's ruling about the Jews, the king replied that he could not. However, he gave Esther and Mordecai permission to write another decree "in the king's name, and seal it with the king's ring: the writing which is written in the king's name, and sealed with the king's ring, may no man reverse" (Esther 8:8).

The women in the king's court are of particular importance in the book of Esther. When the king called for new virgins to be brought before him as candidates for queen, the women were not voluntarily offering themselves. "Let the king appoint officers in all the provinces of his kingdom, that they may gather together all the fair young virgins unto Shushan the palace..." (Esther 2:3). Families were not given the right of refusal. There is no indication or reason to believe that either Mordecai or Esther sought this "opportunity." The women who were taken were virgins. Only one woman could be crowned queen. Once each woman spent her night with the king, she became part of the king's harem and property of the king for life. In her book *Leading Lessons*, Dr. Jeanne Porter writes:

> A harem literally means "sanctuary" and was usually a secluded house or part of a house allotted to women. Notwithstanding our Western stereotypical perception of the harem as a place of beautiful, sensual maidens, the harem was the place in polygamous cultures where all of the women—wives, concubines, female relatives, and servants—lived.[7]

While Persian culture was male-dominated and women's rights were restricted, some women had more freedom than modern readers might think. For example, "Persian royal wives" could attend banquets and accompany "the king on hunts and even military campaigns."[8] Concubines had fewer rights than primary wives, but they were not necessarily of low social class. The women who resided in the king's harem came from various backgrounds. Some were the daughters of other kings with whom alliances had been made. Despite the fact they might never be called to the king's bed again, the concubines in the palace were there for the exclusive pleasure of the king and were often given their own quarters and attendants. The harem was guarded by eunuchs, men who had been castrated to assure they would not touch the women.

The Obliteration of Identity

Conquering nations showed their dominance by changing the names of their captives. This explains why Esther's name was changed from Hadassah. Christians are most familiar with the name changes found in Dan 1:7 and 4:7: Belteshazzar (Daniel), Hananiah (Shadrach), Mishael (Meshach), and Azariah (Abed-nego). While the captives were allowed to use their abilities in the service of the conquering power (Dan 2:48), the name change was a public declaration that the heritage and nationality of the conquered people had been subsumed by the conquering king. Second, and more importantly, the name was a public display of the defeat of the gods of the nation taken under siege. The new name was based on the name of one of the gods of the conquering nation.[9] In Dan 4:8, King Nebuchadnezzar says: "Daniel came in before me, whose name was Belteshazzar, according to the name of my god, and in whom is the spirit of the holy gods." This change in name was particularly offensive to the Jews, who worshiped Jehovah as the one true God. Being named after a false god or forced to pay homage to an idol was the height of degradation and shame. Being called by the captor's name was an ever-present reminder that their lives, skills, and worship belonged to the conquering nation.

It is unclear from the text when it was determined that Esther's identity as a Jew should be hidden. Rabbinical literature has sought to explain why and how this was done, but the question is unresolved. It could be that the royal summons was a factor. It stands to reason that the nations and people who were forced to co-exist in the Persian Empire would have had a tumultuous history of alliances and hatreds. Possible tensions among the conquered subjects, the Persian officials, and any persons desiring to gain the king's favor would have made the decision to conceal Esther's heritage and background the best option since doing otherwise could have proven deadly. Another explanation offered by Rabbis is that life in the palace was contrary to all things Jewish. To maintain the honor of her people, Esther was to keep a low profile as a matter of modesty.[10]

Generational Hatred and a Dangerous Life

Mordecai refused to bow to Haman because Haman was an Amalekite, a member of a nation with whom Israel had been enemies since the days of Joshua. Haman's nationality is mentioned in Esther 3:1, where he is referred to as "the Agagite." Agag was the former king of the Amalekites. Exodus 17:8-16 records the battle between Israel and the Amalekites under Joshua and Moses:

> [8]Then came Amalek, and fought with Israel in Rephidim.
> [9]And Moses said unto Joshua, Choose us out men, and go out, fight with Amalek: to morrow I will stand on the top of the hill with the rod of God in mine hand.

¹⁰So Joshua did as Moses had said to him, and fought with Amalek: and Moses, Aaron, and Hur went up to the top of the hill.

¹¹And it came to pass, when Moses held up his hand, that Israel prevailed: and when he let down his hand, Amalek prevailed.

¹²But Moses hands were heavy; and they took a stone, and put it under him, and he sat thereon; and Aaron and Hur stayed up his hands, the one on the one side, and the other on the other side; and his hands were steady until the going down of the sun.

¹³And Joshua discomfited Amalek and his people with the edge of the sword.

¹⁴And the LORD said unto Moses, Write this for a memorial in a book, and rehearse it in the ears of Joshua: for I will utterly put out the remembrance of Amalek from under heaven.

¹⁵And Moses built an altar, and called the name of it Jehovah-nissi:

16 For he said, Because the LORD hath sworn that the LORD will have war with Amalek from generation to generation.

First Samuel 15 reports that when Saul was ordered by God through the prophet Samuel to annihilate the Amalekites, he failed to do so. For his transgression, the crown was taken from him. In 1 Samuel 30, David and the Amalekites engaged in a viciously bloody battle. This history of violent social, political, and religious hatred did not abate over the centuries.

Recognizing the confrontations between Israel and the Amalekites puts the events of the book of Esther into perspective. While there were many Jews in Shushan, Mordecai appears to be the only Jew who ignored the mandate to bow before Haman. Haman's decision to kill all Jews seems excessive. Talmudic literature offers several reasons for the venomous response of Haman to Mordecai's refusal to bow.[11] However, the confrontation is really a matter of honor and shame for both men as each seeks to defend his heritage and his national god.

Haman immediately knew why Mordecai did not bow. His use of deception to manipulate the king to approve the genocide is proof of the racial, political, and religious enmity between them:

> Then Haman approached King Xerxes and said, "There is a *certain race* of people scattered through all the provinces of your empire *who keep themselves separate* from everyone else. Their laws are *different* from those of any other people, and *they refuse to obey* the laws of the king. So it is not in the king's interest to let them live. If it please the king, issue a decree that they be destroyed..." (Esther 3:8 NLT).

Haman sought official approval from the king to kill these people who he claimed were separate and refused to obey the king's laws. The Jews had not disobeyed the law of the king, but they were known to keep the laws of Jehovah. Haman's actions were aimed at striking down these people and shaming their God, who would, he thought, be unable to protect them.

Mordecai made his stand for Jehovah with his refusal to bow to the archenemy of God and the nation of Israel,

God's chosen people. Mordecai boldly stated that he was a Jew (Esther 3:4) to bring shame to Haman and honor to Jehovah.[12] His declaration of his race and his God was his stand for the honor of the Jewish people.

The hostilities between Mordecai and Haman clarify Esther's situation. This tension of shame and honor explains why Mordecai positioned himself at the gate on a daily basis to see how Esther was faring. During her preparation, Mordecai's presence would have been a source of strength and hope, especially because she could not reveal herself to be a Jew. When the plot to destroy the Jews was revealed, Mordecai urged Esther's to defend the honor of Jehovah and her people. Failure to do so would have resulted in her shame.

Hollywood has repeatedly depicted Esther and King Ahasuerus as main characters in a love story. The account is better understood in the context of its political, social, and religious tensions. The dangers to Esther were real, and the courage she exhibited was miraculous. Once Esther understood the need for honor, she declared, "If I perish." Her declaration was not for dramatic effect. Esther realized that if God did not protect her, her statement would have described her fate. The palace was a dangerous place; one's life could be taken in a single moment.

GOD IN HER LIFE

The primary criticism of the book of Esther is that it does not mention the name of God or make any definitive and overt references to God or the Hebrew faith. That does not mean Esther's life does not reveal an understanding and reliance upon Jehovah as her God and deliverer.

God's Favor and Purpose

Throughout her life, Esther found favor with God. Orphaned in a foreign land, God's favor allowed her to be adopted as the daughter of her uncle Mordecai. Given the outcome of events years later, we must conclude that it was God's favor that had Esther taken to the palace for the consideration of the king. God placed Hegai, the keeper of the women who were being prepared to meet the king, in a position to influence the lives of these women. God's favor led Hegai to pour all of his influence into the care of Esther.

> [Esther] pleased (Hegai), and she obtained kindness of him; and he speedily gave her her things for purification, with such things as belonged to her, and seven maidens, which were meet to be given her, out of the king's house: and he preferred her and her maids unto the best place of the house of the women. (Esther 2:9)

God's purpose for Esther's life is revealed in one of the most famous conversations in the Bible. When faced with the threat of annihilation of their people, Mordecai explains to Esther that it is time for her to reveal herself. His statement proclaimed his basic faith in God to rule over all situations: "Who knoweth whether thou art come to the kingdom for such a time as this (Esther 4:14)?" To this, Esther replied, "If I perish, I perish" (v. 16). Until this time, Esther had held her peace regarding her religious and racial background, but Mordecai made the case that the purpose and timing of her revelation were now clear.

"If you keep quiet at a time like this, deliverance and relief for the Jews will arise from some other place, but you and your relatives will die" (v.14 NLT). For Mordecai, Jehovah was the deliverer of Israel and would deliver them from all enemies. If Esther refused to declare herself, she was standing with the enemy of God and her people. Esther's actions revealed her understanding of God's favor. Her purpose then was to bring honor to Jehovah.

God's Favor, Faithfulness, and Direction

God had always shown favor in Esther's life. Her adoption by Mordecai assured that she would learn the tenets of her Hebrew heritage. At his knee, she had learned of Israel's history and deliverance. She no doubt learned that there was hope in Jehovah that could not be abated or denied. As queen, Esther was reminded by her uncle that they had hidden her racial identity for a reason, but she was not to deny the God of Israel when it was time to defend their faith. Haman's decree was against Jews everywhere – "scattered through all of the provinces of the (Persian) empire." No hamlet or hovel would be unturned in Haman's quest. "Don't think for a moment that because you're in the palace you will escape when all other Jews are killed" (Esther 4:13 NLT). Mordecai never doubted that God would be victorious and His people avenged. He maintained his faith in the Lord of hosts; thus, so did Esther.

Lillian Klein points out that Esther's actions move the encounter from a human challenge to one of obedience to the authority of God.[13] Haman's threat was a challenge to the faithfulness of God and the faithfulness of God's people to their Lord. His intimidation was a reminder of the historic wars between Israel and the Amalekites. This was not a human battle. It was a battle of a nation whose identity was steeped in its faith in Jehovah. It was a war between the God of Israel and the gods of the Amalekites.

The Power of Prayer and Fasting

Once the decree regarding the Jews was made, Mordecai continued to come to the palace daily. However, now his presence was a demonstration of distress. In keeping with Jewish traditions of mourning, Mordecai donned sackcloth and ashes, and wailed loudly. He was mourning because of the threat of death for the Jews and the affront to God by Haman. His public display led Esther to seek entrance to the king's chamber to make her petition. Knowing she could not enter his chamber without an invitation, Esther called a fast for all of the Jews (Esther 4:16). Determined to have even more people call on her God, Esther engaged her servants in this prayer ritual.

Esther was the queen, but like her predecessor, Queen Vashti, she could be removed at any moment and for any reason. It took boldness to include the servants in the palace in her fasting ritual. It is likely her servants came from various backgrounds, cultures, and religions. The fact that Esther involved them is an indication she had found favor with them and that they were learning from her who Jehovah was. While prayer is not specifically noted in the text, it must be assumed from the context. If the fast was to accomplish its aim, then the servants had to pray to Jehovah. No false god would do. This worship and petition must be wholly acceptable to the God of Israel if honor was to be restored.

On the third day of the fast, Esther donned her royal robes and stood near the king's house. When God directed King Ahasuerus' vision, he extended the golden scepter giving Esther the invitation she needed. God gave Esther the wisdom to know how to appeal to the king and how to reveal the plot against her people. God's favor was again with Esther as the king granted her requests. In the end, God saved His people and vanquished the enemy. Honor was restored to God and the Jews.

WHAT HER LIFE SPEAKS

In many ways, Esther's life seems so far removed from ours that we wonder what practical guidance her life can speak to Christians today. Our circumstances may be different, but Esther's life has a story to tell and advice to give. Her experiences are more universal than we might believe.

Concept 1: Faith Tested Is True Faith

"Faith is the confidence that what we hope for will actually happen; it gives us assurance about things we cannot see" (Heb 11:1 NLT). Faith is not wishful thinking. It is the reliance we have that God will deliver. Neither Esther nor Mordecai waivered in their belief that the Sovereign God would honor His covenant with His people. They had faith in God because He had faithfully delivered them from the hands of their enemies throughout history.

As Christians, we must have confidence that God's Word and promises are true. It is easy to talk about trusting God in the good times. It is even politically correct to give God honor among people of like faith. However, faith in God in the hard times, when adversity hits or death is pending, is another matter. Our exercise of faith reveals the evidence of our character. Hebrews 11:2 says, "Through their faith, the people in days of old earned a good reputation." Esther exercised her faith and stood by her beliefs in the face of fear, hatred, and the threat of death. As Christians, we must be ready to stand in faith even when it is difficult or unpopular. We must be willing to maintain our faith even when our senses and our situations want us to give up. The Holy Spirit is our guide and our help even in times of real trouble. We can say we have faith but only when it is tested can we be seen as faithful people.

Concept 2: We Have the Assurance of God's Protection and Deliverance

Speaking of God's protection and deliverance is much different from being assured of God's deliverance. It is that "blessed assurance" that sustains us and demonstrates our faith to the world. Esther was able to influence history because she had the assurance that God would act. The issue for Christians today is that our memories often fail us. We forget what God has done, and we develop our own "safety nets." Whether we turn to people rather than prayer or anger rather than God's Word, the outcome is generally disappointment and regret that we didn't trust God.

The words of the hymn "What a Friend We Have in Jesus" remind us of the consequence of forgetting to rely on God: "O what peace we often forfeit. O what needless pain we bear all because we do not carry everything to God in prayer." The Lord has provided three reminders of His faithfulness. We simply need to use them.

The first is the truth of the Bible. Undergirding our faith is the knowledge that "All scripture is given by inspiration of God, and is profitable for doctrine, for reproof, for correction, for instruction in righteousness" (2 Tim 3:16). When we give attention to the spiritual discipline of prayerfully reading the Bible as a devotional practice, we learn how God has presented himself faithfully in the affairs of humankind. As we move from just reading to studying the Bible, our understanding of God's faithfulness, majesty, and power is enhanced. The Bible records the history of God's actions. The accounts of the heroines of faith such as Esther have been preserved to provide the revelation of God's faithfulness through time. They are reminders of God's help in the midst of struggle.

The second reminder of God's deliverance is personal experience. The actions of the Lord in the past are the foundation for believing His promises for the future. What you have seen the Lord do in your life is proof of His ability to act in your life again. Have you ever faced a crisis and called on God for deliverance? Did He deliver you? Have you cried out for His protection and seen His hand provide the mercy you needed? How often have you wanted a particular outcome only to discover that while God may not have given it to you in the way you expected, His outcome was better than you could have imagined. God's deliverance in the past is the reminder that He holds our futures in His hand. Our task is to trust that His plan for the future is what we need—even if it is not what we think we want.

We need not experience every tragedy and triumph to know that God's hand is at work in our lives. The final assurance of God's ability and power is the consistency of His actions in the lives of others. Another hymn provides a reminder: "It is no secret what God can do. What He's done for others, He'll do for you." The Lord is so consistent that we can have faith in Him based on what He has done for others. He has delivered those people of faith who are in our families, churches, and communities. Their testimonies are our witness of God's power and desire to deliver us.

Whether we recall what God did for us personally, reflect on what He has done for others, or hold fast to the biblical record of faith, we cannot deny this "evidence of things not seen" (Heb 11:1). It is our assurance that God's deliverance and protection are ours.

Concept 3: Spiritual Discipline Is Necessary for Faithful Living

How do we learn to have faith? How do we grow strong in our reliance upon God? The practical exercise of faith, particularly in the face of conflict or trouble does not occur by osmosis. When Esther called a fast, it was not because she just had an idea "out of the blue." It was because she knew fasting and prayer to be disciplines that could put her heart in tune with God's will. Esther's declaration of "if I perish" was filled with anxiety. Nevertheless, she sought God through the practice of spiritual discipline, and He gave her comfort and confidence.

It is true that when the Holy Spirit comes upon us we are given divine power to rely on and obey God (Acts 1:8), but knowing when and how to use that power is learned over time. Many books have been written on spiritual disciplines that include reading and studying the Bible, singing hymns, sharing our testimonies, worshiping, fasting, and practicing moments of silence before God. By exercising these disciplines every day, we learn to depend on God.

In the New Testament, the Apostles had been with Jesus and had received His instructions, but they didn't know what to do following the Crucifixion. Acts 1:14 says that they were in constant prayer. Prayer is a spiritual discipline. It aligns hearts and minds to God's will. Prayer provides a time to pour out our concerns and fears. It is a process through which we are encouraged by the Holy Spirit. When we share our requests for prayer, receive the prayers of others, or pray for those in need, we are encouraging one another also.

Just fifty days later, on the Day of Pentecost, the new believers were given divine power to respond in faith to the leading of the Holy Spirit. By the time we read Acts 2:42, we see the Apostles and the disciples who gathered with them engaged in ministries that were both powerful and empowering. They shared the gospel, engaged in fellowship, partook of the Lord's Supper, and gave themselves over to prayer. All of these are disciplines—methods of training our hearts to hear God and our minds to follow the leading of the Holy Spirit.

Like Esther and the Apostles, we are not without trepidation, but through the regular exercise of spiritual discipline, we are able to live out our faith in the good times and the difficult situations. Through spiritual discipline, we learn to know God's leading. We learn to accept His will even in the most trying situations. We learn to wait patiently for His grace. Above all, the exercise of spiritual discipline prepares us so that when our faith is tested we are able to walk in the destiny God has prepared for us.

Hearing Esther

WHAT YOUR LIFE SPEAKS

Speak Your Truth
1. Esther faced her challenge head-on. What challenge are you facing?
2. When your faith is challenged, what do you do?

Focus Your Faith
1. Actions such as prayer, fasting, daily devotions, memorizing Scriptures are a few of the spiritual disciplines available to Christians. What spiritual disciplines help you grow in faith? Which are least familiar to you? How can you become more comfortable with those disciplines?
2. Esther realized she must do the Lord's bidding rather than remain in her own "safe space." How is your faith calling you from your comfort zone?

USING YOUR VOICE

Ponder
1. Esther engaged her servants and all of the Jews in Shushan to join her in fasting and prayer. Have you ever fasted? Search for Scriptures involving fasting to learn more about this discipline. Also, speak with your pastor or a Christian who has fasted to gain additional insight.
2. Esther called on many people to join her in prayer. Who do you call as prayer partners in your spiritual walk?

3. Esther felt that she had "come to the kingdom for such a time as this." This is a description of her call to make a difference in the world. What do you think is your call from the Lord to make a difference?

Pray

1. Esther prayed about the fate of the Jews. Make a list of the actions, people, and circumstances you need to take to God in prayer.

2. A common format for prayer is found in the acronym ACTS. Write or pray a prayer that incorporates these four actions:
   A – Adore God
   C – Confess your sins and faults
   T – Thank God for the many blessing He has given you
   S – State your requests for yourself and others

Practice

1. Mordecai helped Esther to move beyond her fear and grow in faith. How can you help someone in your family, church, or larger community do the same?

2. Twice, the king asked Esther what she wanted. Each time she had a ready answer. Identify what you want for your family or community, then put it into words and develop a plan to accomplish it. Be prepared to share your insight and vision with others.

Vashti

THE BOOK OF ESTHER

SOME PEOPLE SEEM TO HAVE IT ALL: money, beauty, fame, and power. While we may think this about people we know, it is usually the description of a celebrity. Queen Vashti fell into that category. She was married to the most powerful man in the world and reaped all the benefits of his wealth. Queen Vashti lived an existence that could only be described as larger than life. But because she also lived in her husband's shadow, her life comes into focus only when we view it through the lens of King Ahasuerus's fortune and position. Nevertheless, Queen Vashti managed to live life on her terms.

SYNOPSIS

Queen Vashti is only mentioned in Esther 1. Her story is embedded in that chapter's account of two separate banquets designed to impress King Ahasuerus's subjects. Esther 1:3 explains that the king's 180-day banquet was for "all his princes and his servants; the power of Persia and Media, the nobles and princes of the provinces, being before him." This feast was followed by a banquet for "all the people that were present in Shushan the palace, both unto great and small, seven days, in the court of the garden of the king's palace" (Esther 1:5). Simultaneously, Queen Vashti took the opportunity to entertain her guests: "the women in the royal house which belonged to King Ahasuerus" (Esther 1:9). We cannot be sure how many women were invited. It is likely they were the wives of the princes the king entertained.

During his banquet, the king ordered that every man should drink as much as he desired. On "the seventh day, when the heart of the king was merry with wine," he sent servants to bring the queen before the gathered and drunken guests. The king had already displayed the jewels, furnishings, vessels, and other artifacts that affirmed his wealth and power. Now he wanted to show off his queen. Queen Vashti refused to attend. No reason is given for her refusal, and the discussion between the queen and the chamberlains is not recorded. We are left simply with a defiant queen and an angry and embarrassed king (Esther 1:8-12).

The king's public request and the queen's public denial were met with a public query regarding what should be done to the disobedient queen. Having been personally offended on the king's behalf, the seven princes suggested that Queen Vashti's actions were an affront not only to the king but also to "*all* the princes, and to *all* the people that are in *all* the provinces of the king Ahasuerus" (v. 16). The advisors portrayed Queen Vashti's actions as inciting a rebellion among "*all* women" in their provinces as well. They predicted that because of the queen's behavior, husbands *everywhere* would be despised, and wives *everywhere* would follow her example (v. 17).

To rectify Queen Vashti's affront to life in the Empire, King Ahasuerus wrote two decrees. The first ruling banished Vashti from the royal court and the king's presence. Her crown and position were to be given to another woman. The second decree demanded that wives honor their husbands (vv. 19-20). These missives were issued in all of the languages of the vast Persian Empire.

LIFE IN HER WORLD

Queen Vashti's presence in the book of Esther is limited to only the first chapter. From that point, the biblical record provides no more information about her. The historic record casts doubt on whether the actual queen's name was Vashti. This begs the question of whether Vashti was really important to the book. After all, it is entitled "Esther" and the remaining nine chapters involve Queen Esther, her uncle Mordecai, and the dreaded Haman. Vashti's presence seems small, and her voice is never heard. We know of her decision only from the report given to the king. These factors might make us think Vashti has nothing to say to modern audiences. We would be wrong. Vashti is a legendary and heroic figure who speaks loudly to women across cultures and generations. Her world was dominated by political alliances and upheaval. While theologians question the veracity of her account, the facts of her world are well documented.

At Home in the Palace

King Ahasuerus's palaces were Vashti's homes. The book of Ezra mentions two of the king's palaces in Ecbatana (Achmetha) and Babylon (Ezra 6:1-2). The city of Shushan, or Susa, is the palatial site of events in the book of Esther. Archeologists have found ruins that certify the city of Shushan had grown to "625 acres" prior to King Ahasuerus taking to the throne. A major canal separated the city's lower and upper banks. Under King Darius, a citadel had been built that included "a monumental gate, and a large palace with two divisions, a three-acre audience hall and a ten-acre residential area with four successive inner courts."[1] The gate of the city was a magnificent structure. It was attached by massive columns to the gatehouse, which stood east of the palace.[2]

The Queen's Influence

The royal women of Persia were permitted to attend banquets with the men; yet, Vashti hosted a separate banquet. The term "feast" describes Queen Vashti's party and implies an abundance of wine and food. The fact that her banquet is not mentioned prominently causes us to wonder whether Queen Vashti often gave banquets for the women. The fact that her banquet is mentioned at all gives us a hint at Vashti's presence and purpose in the kingdom.[3] The queen obviously had influence in the lives of the women of the court. Just as the men were impressed with the king's wealth and generosity, the women would have been grateful for the queen's invitation and attention and possibly mesmerized by her demeanor, voice, or knowledge of culture, politics, and the affairs of the home. Whatever the case, Queen Vashti was apparently quite charismatic.

Because of her influential position and personality, Vashti's refusal to appear before the king's court was seen as an insult to the king's power. Members of the court used this occasion to send a warning to women across the land and a message to men everywhere. At the urging of his princes, the king issued a royal standard for female behavior in the home. The harshness and swiftness of the decrees infer the level of Queen Vashti's popularity and influence. The edicts were aimed at restoring the honor of husbands of all ages and stations (great and small). The royal missives as dictated by the king's princes declared that every woman should honor her husband. They also decreed that "every man should be ruler over his own household, using his native tongue" (Esther 1:20-22). The decrees, written in the husbands' native tongues, were intended to give men throughout the Empire the security of being revered as the heads of their houses. This was a direct affront to the influence of the queen upon the wives.

Life with King Ahasuerus

King Ahasuerus's actions provide a backdrop to Queen Vashti's life. The first chapter of Esther describes a king and a kingdom that were out of control and self-indulgent. According to Rabbi Eidensohn, Torah attributes the king's wealth to treasures confiscated from Babylon.[4] The extent of the king's possessions is seen in part through the frequency of dinners hosted at the palace. The ten banquets mentioned in the book of Esther give insight into the king's boastful and impetuous personality.

King Ahasuerus also appears to be easily influenced by his appointees to the royal court. The custom of gaining the consensus of key princes in the Empire may have served the king well as a military strategy. It did not succeed as a way "to rule in his own house" (Esther 1:22). When King Ahasuerus asked his confidantes to mete out the punishment to Queen Vashti, he was not responding as a husband to an altercation with his wife. He was demonstrating his concern for how he appeared to others. His decision to oust Vashti was a rash one based on the advice of men who used her refusal to appear before them as an opportunity to press a larger agenda. We get this understanding from the regret the king projected in Esther 2:1 when his "fury had subsided, (and) he remembered Vashti and what she had done and what he had decreed about her." His pining for Vashti was so great that in verse 2, "the king's personal attendants proposed, 'Let a search be made for beautiful young virgins for the king.'"

An examination of King Ahasuerus's responses to others sheds light on the life Queen Vashti would have had. In order to appreciate the extent of the king's irrational behavior, we must look beyond chapter 1. In Esther 3:8-12, Haman, a chief official, presents his request to massacre the entire Jewish population of Persia. Without asking any questions, King Ahasuerus set his seal upon the decree. In Esther 5, Queen Esther was able to manipulate the king's impulsive and sensual desire to gain an audience with him by simply positioning herself outside his window. Esther's request that King Ahasuerus and Haman attend a banquet was met with the king's urgent call for Haman to appear (Esther 5:5). In chapter 7, Queen Esther revealed Haman's guilt in plotting to kill her and her people. The king's fury caused him to accuse Haman of attempting to rape his wife and therefore usurp his throne (Esther 7:8). Haman is immediately ordered to be hanged, his house given to Queen Esther, and his position given to Mordecai (Esther 8:1-2). Despite the fact that all the tension in the book of Esther is caused by his impetuous laws, King Ahasuerus extended permission for Esther and Mordecai to write a new decree as *they* saw fit. Again he asked no questions and was not concerned with the impact of their decision on the people of the Empire (Esther 8:5-10).

In each instance, King Ahasuerus's behavior was rash and egotistical. He set the royal seal upon documents without concern to the matters they conveyed. He ordered banishment and death when things appeared to be an affront to him or when others told him he had been insulted and disrespected. He promoted people and bestowed honor haphazardly. Despite the vastness of the Empire, King Ahasuerus appeared to wield his power impetuously. Life as King Ahasuerus's wife would have been taxing for Vashti and constantly held the possibility of disaster or death either for her or someone else.

When Queen Vashti's personality is viewed in light of King Ahasuerus's temperament, we see the crux of the conflict in her life. While Queen Vashti enjoyed the king's wealth and her position, her self-assurance placed her in opposition to her husband. Whether she overstepped by refusing to attend the king's banquet or demonstrated dignity through her refusal to be "displayed" is not known. What we see is the calm demeanor of the queen in the face of the king's impetuous nature. Perhaps Queen Vashti's real "crime" was her display of confidence in the midst of chaos.

GOD IN HER LIFE

God has never eliminated women. Throughout the Old Testament, we see God positioning women to change the tenor of the times. Sarah's influence over Abraham led to the birth of a second nation through Hagar (Gen 16). Deborah's influence and guidance as a judge made the difference for Barak in the attack on Jabin, the king of Canaan (Judg 4 and 5). Hannah's gift of Samuel to the work of the Lord led to the re-shaping of Israel in preparation for a king (1 Sam 1). Bathsheba's actions were critical in David's decision to place Solomon on the throne (1 Kings 1). While each woman in the Bible lived in a male-dominated society, their presence indicated God's placement of women in the vortex of national direction. The actions of women in touching the hearts and minds of leaders often served God's eternal plan. Queen Vashti was such a woman.

Like other women in the Old Testament, little is said about Queen Vashti's impact, but examining the events related to her reveal her power as a leader of women. Queen Vashti was not a Jew. She had no Jewish influence in her life. She was an idol worshiper; it is impossible to assign to her any connection to the God of Israel. We can, however, identify her as part of God's divine plan to save the Jews from extinction.

Vashti: God's Vessel for Transforming the Women's Quarters

Despite her non-Jewish background, the key to finding the influence of God in Queen Vashti's life lies in Esther 1:9, which states, "Queen Vashti gave a banquet for the women in the royal palace of King Xerxes" (NLT). This seemingly innocuous statement is important in God's plan. The women of Persia came from every part of the known world—from India to Egypt. Queen Vashti's gathering apparently gave voice to this diverse group of women.

We can only speculate at the banter that might have occurred at the queen's banquet. Since the primary concerns of women were child-bearing and taking care of their households, guidance for childcare and tending to husbands would likely have been topics of discussion. The women probably told stories to encourage those who were despondent or to make each other glad over some event or situation. Secrets of personal grooming and health as well would have been shared in the women's quarters. By hosting this women-only event, Queen Vashti helped them to recognize their own voices and the importance of contributing their voices to the affairs of their lives. In the safety of her banquet, women were free to speak and to think about what their lives meant.

If we examine the reaction of the princes to Queen Vashti's refusal to come to the king's banquet, we notice

their concern was for wives to be obedient and totally submissive to their husbands. To the king's advisors, Vashti's
refusal to attend the king's banquet was a threat to family
life. The men were apparently fearful that Queen Vashti's actions and attitudes would be replicated by—or at
least admired by—other women. What the king's advisors
feared, and what was likely happening through Queen
Vashti's gathering of "royal women," was transformation.
If we put speculation about their conversation aside, we
are left to assume that what ever Queen Vashti did in her
banquet, taught women to think differently.

The decrees designed to banish Queen Vashti attest
to the strength of her influence. By issuing such harsh and
immediate laws against Vashti, the leaders essentially ad-
mitted that her style of hospitality was fostering a powerful network of women. While their intent was to abate
the uprising of wives, their declarations were too late.
Queen Vashti had changed the atmosphere in the wom-
en's quarters. She had apparently nurtured relationships
and strengthened conversations. The edicts designed to
stop her interference in home life reveal how God used
Queen Vashti to set the tone for unity and support in the
women's quarters.

Vashti: God's Conduit for Global Change

The decrees against Vashti were used by the Persian princes to provide a global call for reform of home life. The laws
against Queen Vashti help us understand her as a guid-
ing figure within the Empire who recognized the importance of her influence and used it to help her royal sisters
discern the power inherent in their roles as mothers and

wives. Her refusal to appear before the king and his guests was an assertion of her power to influence the affairs of the Empire.

The emphasis in the book of Esther is the salvation of the Jews. There can be little doubt that Vashti's presence laid the groundwork for Queen Esther's triumph over Haman. Queen Esther came to the throne four years after Vashti's banishment; yet, the tone set by Vashti prepared a place for Esther to learn the importance of her own voice. When Mordecai asked Esther to go to the king for the Jewish people, she originally was hesitant (Esther 4). As Queen Esther gave her attention to Mordecai's pleas, perhaps the stories she had heard from women who had been in Vashti's presence years earlier rang in Esther's heart and gave her the courage to confront the king. After all, if Queen Vashti could stand up against tyranny for a small thing, Queen Esther could stand for her God and her people.

Queen Esther's preparation to go before the king employed traditions from her Jewish heritage as well as her knowledge of life in the royal court. Queen Esther's first action was to call a three-day fast among "all the Jews that are present in Shushan..." But Esther's plan included both Jews and non-Jews. "I also and my maidens will fast likewise..." Her confidence in this eclectic group of prayer warriors was so strong that she declared, "If I perish, I perish" (Esther 4:16). Death was a great possibility for Esther. So what gave Esther the assurance that a group of women from various backgrounds would stand with her? She had not revealed her Jewish heritage before. What made her certain that asking for the participation of non-Jews would not jeopardize the plan and cost the lives of her people? What had occurred in the women's quarters that enabled Queen Esther to enlist the help of her non-Jewish servants? Queen Vashti happened! Vashti taught the women that sisterhood was important, that it went beyond racial and social norms. Vashti demonstrated that women could be influential; they could support one another and the causes they held dear. Through Vashti, God prepared the atmosphere of victory for the Jews and a global change in their fate.

WHAT HER LIFE SPEAKS

Issues faced by women today include family relationships, education, and employment. Women are concerned about violence and abuse, world issues, health, and personal spiritual journeys. Queen Vashti's life speaks to each category because her life challenges women to recognize their abilities and moral fiber. Queen Vashti's presence in the book of Esther still encourages women to be supportive of one another as we use our voices in our personal spheres of influence.

Concept 1: We are Strengthened When We Support One Another

By gathering women, Vashti demonstrated that the comradery of women has always been important. The women who came to Vashti's gathering were wives of the princes and governors of the Empire. Their responsibilities involved care for their children and their households including the slaves and concubines who lived there. It meant being wives who were fitting companions for their husbands and the positions their husbands held. It was the norm for Vashti's time for women to be married, and it was deemed a disgrace for women not to be mothers. Vashti met with women who were married, in many cases through arranged or political marriages.

Things have changed. Modern women are more comfortable with singleness and with not having children. Women no longer fall into one category. Women's lives are complicated, and no lifestyle should be considered better than another. Still, women struggle to do "everything." Whether they work outside of the home, run their own companies, or provide home schooling for their children, women need and welcome the support of other women. When women's circumstances are similar, their networking helps them share the burdens and garner sustaining advice. Even when women come from a variety of situations and have vastly different concerns, their gathering creates an atmosphere that is strengthening and encouraging.

Hebrews 10:23-25 (NIV), gives excellent advice to the church on supporting one another:

Let us hold tightly without wavering to the hope we affirm, for God can be trusted to keep his promise. Let us think of ways to motivate one another to acts of love and good works. And let us not neglect our meeting together, as some people do, but encourage one another, especially now that the day of his return is drawing near.

While Hebrews is clearly about assembly in the worship setting, it carries an admission that unity and support are critical to our lives regardless of our social obligations, personal responsibilities, or age. Vashti's example, coupled with the advice in Hebrews, should encourage every woman to make her way to the women's quarters. Every woman must find the time to ferret out the space to join other women in the refreshing joy of sisterhood.

Concept 2: We Each Have Spheres of Influence

Even by modern standards, the women who came to Vashti's banquet were busy women with busy lives. Some may have been social climbers or even the thrust behind their husbands' positions of power. They were the confidantes to their husbands, which also meant they had the power to soothe as well as the power to incite action. We repeatedly see biblical examples of women who influenced their husband's lives. Women's negative influences include the actions of Jezebel in taking Naboth's garden for her sulking husband, King Ahab (1 Kings 21). Positive influences include Abigail, who changed the fate of her husband against David's wrath (1 Sam 25).

The influence of women as wives and mothers has not diminished. Women are still concerned with protecting their families and serving in their roles as caregivers and counselors in their homes and other relationships. Whether women are married or single, they cannot escape their role in the financial health of their households. Today, women are also influential in the workplace and in the government. Obviously, changes have come as women have been elected to political office or elevated to positions in the corporate world. Unfortunately, women's roles are still not equal to that of men, and the glass ceiling does not seem to be moving quickly or, in some cases, at all. Still, women are apt to find their means of influence in any position they hold.

As Christians, our influence is not only critical but mandated. In His Sermon on the Mount (Matt 5:13-16), Jesus told His followers they were to be the salt and the light that leads others to our heavenly Father. Our role as salt and light means we are to set the tone for the practical and daily engagement of those around us. Christian women set the tone for their households and for their lives in public spaces. Everyone influences how other people see them. For Christians, this tends to cause neighbors, co-workers, and family members to examine their own actions and attitudes in our presence. This is not punitive or accusatory. In fact, it may be unconscious. People may tend to think about their choice of words or choose not to give the most "colorful" examples to prove their point just because they respect the person before them. Even though the concerns of Christian women are the same as women of all cultures, faiths, and age groups, when women demonstrate spiritual and moral integrity, people recognize the salt in the room. Salt changes everything, and light presents a presence that cannot be ignored. This only happens, however, when a Christian's actions are authentic.

Concept 3: Our Authenticity Is a Powerful Witness and Influence

It is critical that every woman find her authentic self. According to Webster, authentic has to do with conforming to or representing essential elements of an original.[5] For

Christians, Jesus Christ is the original because He is "the author and finisher of our faith" (Hebrews 12:2). Christian women are authentic when they stand for the principles of God in a manner that does not compromise their God-given personalities and gifts.

Tradition is a powerful impetus for action, but tradition can become rote if we only mimic the past. In Vashti's case, tradition held that she was to be obedient to her husband regardless of how degrading or detrimental that obedience was. She chose not to follow tradition. Instead, she examined the command in light of the relationship she had established with the women and the person she had become as she understood her position as a leader. Each of us should seek to understand the reasons behind social and family traditions and examine them in light of our Christian witness. Consider this true story shared by a woman at a women's retreat. At twelve years old, she attended a church service with a friend. She recalled wearing a pair of multicolored shoes that her favorite aunt had just given her. At the church she noticed people looking at her shoes with frowns. It turned out that the church held a tradition that only allowed members to wear blue, black, brown and white. She had enjoyed the worship service but never returned to the church. Years later, as an adult, she visited a city aquarium. While looking at the brightly colored fish, the memory of that church came back. She had walked away from the church bothered by that tradition, but upon looking at the fish, she laughed and said, "Clearly God doesn't have a problem with colors." That tradition had no scriptural or real world connection. It was not an authentic representation of what it means to be a Christian. Consequently, it only served to confuse the young girl who was seeking God.

The authentic voice is not found in our unredeemed past. When we stand in the light of Christ's redemptive power, we should no longer respond to situations based on our "old" selves. If we are "new creations" in Christ, we must examine our attitudes and actions in light of Jesus' influence in our lives (2 Corinthians 5:17). Our authenticity, therefore, reflects our response to God's grace. The example of the unforgiving servant presented in Matthew 18:21-35 describes how our response must demonstrate the compassion that God has shown us. Likewise, dogged adherence to our family histories or replication of the mannerisms and actions of others can interfere with our effort to be authentic. When we reflect on who God is calling us to be individually, we open ourselves to being authentic in every aspect of our lives. In this way, we find our "true north" which encompasses the values and ideals we gleaned from family and life experiences, but also reflects our growth in Christ. No doubt there was a time when Vashti responded as any woman in her time would have; but once she realized that her life had changed, her response reflected "the new" Vashti. Her example encourages us to be authentic in our leadership and our response to the actions of others.

Concept 4: We Must Recognize the Importance of Our Integrity

Vashti's behavior has been long viewed by women as a standard for integrity. The men at the king's banquet had been drinking to their fill for seven days. We have no idea of what the king meant by showing her beauty, but his only request was for her crown to be on her head. It could be that Vashti sensed the trouble that would come from her appearance before a throng of drunken men. It could be that the queen was not anxious to be presented as an object and that she felt the king's request disrespected her position as his wife and queen of the Empire. Perhaps, too, her royal position gave her the courage to claim her personal sense of worth. Whatever the reason, Vashti's actions remind us that we must think through every situation, not just for the moment but for the long run. Thinking beyond an immediate pleasure or desire provides time to consider the consequences of our actions.

A few years ago, people appropriated a statement from the early 1900s that asked, "What would Jesus do?" That question may appear trite, but it carries a message that undergirds our decisions regarding integrity. It also raises questions about our actions, particularly in times of crisis and major decisions. What benefit does our embrace of the kingdom of God bring to our families, our society, and our life choices? As citizens of the kingdom of God, what ethical standards and moral values are evident in our decision-making processes? How do our attitudes and conversations reflect our faith as Christians? How do our actions in the church, our families, and our society present a proclamation of our faith and testimony of belief? What would Jesus do? He always acted with integrity and authenticity. We must also.

Vashti met with the women because she felt the need to encourage them. She refused to go to the banquet because she felt that doing so was damaging in some way.

As Christians, we must examine the parameters of our actions based on the Word of God and our faith in Him. Then we must be willing to act when God calls us to do so. We must have the courage to follow God's standard as the bar for integrity and authenticity if we wish to influence our world.

Times change. Styles change. Customs, cultures, human standards, and world crises change. But God's Word and His standard of spiritual and personal integrity for those who are called by the name of Christ do not change. Women of every age group, socio-economic class, and cultural background have something to contribute to the "women's quarters." When individual women put aside ambition and power, and determine what the right thing is for their stand as authentic Christians, they will find themselves with Vashti in the space where integrity is born.

Hearing Vashti

WHAT YOUR LIFE SPEAKS

Speak Your Truth

1. Right or wrong, the princes and governors had an opinion of Queen Vashti. How do you think others see you? Are you pleased or displeased with their perception? What can you do to reinforce or change how you are perceived? Should you?

2. Women need the support of other women. List reasons why such support is important to you.

Focus Your Faith

1. Make a list of the places and situations over which you have influence. Then examine Matthew 5:13-16 and other Bible passages to see what practical advice they give for becoming a more influential Christian.

2. We all have public and private lives. Integrity lies in having a public persona that is not counter to your private self. Are your public and private lives ever in conflict? How? Why?

USING YOUR VOICE

Ponder

1. Vashti provided "safe space" for women to support one another. Where is your safe space? Who do you turn to for support?

2. If you are an overcomer in an area such as abuse, care-

giving, health challenges, addiction, or another area, consider how you can give support to others who are facing similar challenges. You may wish to discuss the possibilities with your pastor or someone who works in that area.

Pray

1. Pray for women who are in your support group.
2. Pray for women who need support but feel they have nowhere to turn.
3. Pray for the girls and young women in your life who are struggling to be authentic Christians.

Practice

1. Hospitals, community organizations, and churches often have support groups and counseling help. Seek out a venue that provides information and help for you or a friend.
2. Get together with friends for a spa day or other outing. If money is a concern, have a "Girl's Night In" where you can watch old movies, give each other pedicures, or share in a potluck meal.

Rahab

JOSHUA 2; JOSHUA 6:17-25; HEBREWS 11:31; JAMES 2:25

A MODERN TRANSLATION of Shakespeare's *Othello* goes like this:

> **Cassio:** "My reputation. My reputation. I have lost my reputation!"
> **Iago:** "You haven't lost it unless you think you have."[1]

Iago's words can be applied to Rahab's outlook on life. The minute we hear her name, we realize that in our minds Rahab has lost her reputation. We cannot be certain of just how negative the term "harlot" was in her day, but we know the horrific connotation of it today. Regardless of how we define reputation, Rahab knew what was important to her. Neither the opinions of others about her lifestyle, nor the restraints society placed on her as a woman, stopped Rahab from achieving great things—even at a great price.

SYNOPSIS

In Joshua 1, Moses was dead. A new chapter was about to begin for the Israelites, who were camped in Shittim on the east side of the Jordan River. It was time to conquer the land that flowed with milk and honey. In Joshua 2, two spies were sent into Jericho to "view the Land." Once inside Jericho, the spies went into a "harlot's house… and lodged there" (Josh 2:1). When the king of Jericho was told of their presence, he immediately sent troops to the house demanding that the men be turned over to the guards.

It is at that point that we meet Rahab, the "harlot" who owned the house where the spies sought refuge. Like the king, Rahab realized the presence of the Israelite spies meant a war was coming and defeat was imminent. The king wanted to stop it; Rahab wanted to be saved from it. Therefore, she hid the spies on her roof and provided them a place to rest for the night. Then she calmly misguided the king's men.

Once the troops were gone, Rahab told the spies that the people of Jericho remembered how the God of Israel defeated Pharaoh. Through her conversation, Rahab revealed the terror their presence provoked in the people of Jericho and "all of the inhabitants of the land" (Josh 2:9). After her admission, she exacted an oath from the Israelite spies that they would not destroy her family when they invaded Jericho. The spies agreed, but required that her house be marked with a symbol—a red cord. With that, Rahab told the spies how to safely return to the Israelite encampment on the other side of the Jordan River.

Several days later, the spies returned to their camp and gave a report to Joshua including their oath to Rahab. In Joshua 3, "all the children of Israel" left the camp in Shittim and moved to the edge of the Jordan River where the plan for taking Jericho was explained.

Before the battle could begin, the children of Israel had work to do. They sanctified themselves unto the Lord (Josh 3:5). They were instructed to build a memorial of stones taken from the River so that future generations would know what God did when they crossed the Jordan to take the Promised Land (Josh 4:1-7). The men who had been born since the escape from Egypt were circumcised and the Passover was observed (Josh 5:7, 10). When preparations were complete, the manna (food) God had provided for the forty years they traveled in the Wilderness, stopped (Josh 5:12). For the first time, Israel ate from the "fruit of the land of Canaan." Joshua issued orders for the march across the Jordan River. With the ark of the Lord leading the people, God would perform a miracle at the River Jordan (Josh 3:11). Finally, "about forty thousand" troops crossed over Jordan ready to defeat the native tribes with the mighty "hand of the Lord" (Josh 4:13, 24).

In chapter 6, the Israelite army marched into Jericho, but the battle was far from traditional. For six days, the Israelites marched around the city walls and blew the rams' horns. On the seventh day, they marched seven times around the city, blew the trumpets, and shouted. It was then that, "the wall fell down flat" (Josh 6:20). The slaughter of Jericho was massive. Israel "utterly destroyed all that was in the city, both man and woman, young and old, and ox, and sheep, and ass, with the edge of the sword" (v. 21). "They burnt the city with fire, and all that was therein: only the silver, and the gold, and the vessels of brass and of iron, they put into the treasury of the house of the LORD" (v. 24).

The two spies, however, led Rahab and her family safely outside the city walls as promised (Josh 6:22-23). Because her wise and heroic stand was pivotal in the battle to take Jericho, Rahab is named in the honor roll of heroes in Hebrews 11. The book of James notes the actions that showed Rahab's faith in God. Rahab is clearly a champion, but her voice and reputation are still hidden behind the epithet "harlot."

Life in Her World

Rahab is one of the people in the Bible whose reputation preceded her actions. At the first mention of her name, she was labeled: Rahab, the prostitute. Although Rahab's deeds are recorded in the book of Joshua and referenced in the New Testament, that marker continues to stain the memory of her actions. Nevertheless, Rahab's life confirms the power of faith.

Rahab's Reputation, Independence, and Concern

To modern Christian minds, the term harlot is an offensive descriptor of this woman of faith because it stands in stark contrast to our concept of a heroine. The term harlot is also contrary to the chastity and sexual purity required of Israelite women. However, the Canaanite nations worshiped multiple gods, not Jehovah of the Israelite people. In pagan cultures, religious practices included worship of the human body, sexuality, and fertility gods. Temple prostitution by men and women was often part of the religious ritual. While Rahab's characterization as a prostitute is never linked to pagan religion, we cannot negate the term from the culture in which Rahab lived. The practice of prostitution was common in Canaanite societies. We cannot tell if these women were looked upon with the same level of disdain and shame we assign prostitutes today. Certainly the temple prostitutes were not. They were considered to be the priests of the fertility gods. Rahab's world was also one where concubines, slaves, and multiple wives were expected to be the objects of sexual pleasure.

Because it is difficult to reconcile the heroism of Rahab and the description of her as "a harlot," we question whether "harlot" is the best word to describe her. While the King James Version of the Bible calls Rahab "an harlot," the New International Version refers to her as "a prostitute." The Complete English Version calls her a prostitute but adds a footnote indicating that "she was possibly an innkeeper."[2] *The Jewish Encyclopedia* states that while rabbinical literature calls Rahab "one who sells food," Talmudic literature accepts that Rahab was a prostitute who became a "sincere proselyte."[3]

Whether she ran a brothel or owned a hostel for weary travels, Rahab was a successful entrepreneur and an independently wealthy woman. The conquest of Jericho began in the spring when "Jordan overfloweth all his banks all the time of harvest" (Josh 3:15). The fact that Rahab had stalks of flax upon her roof (Josh 2:6) indicates that she was processing the recently harvested crop, not simply storing it. While we focus on the health benefits of flaxseed today, in ancient societies flax was most valuable because it could be woven into cloth.[4] The amount of flax on her roof (enough to hide two adult men) indicates how large her roof was and how much flax she had. Once processed, the flax would be dyed. The cord or "scarlet thread" that Rahab lowered from her window was likely made of flax. If she was in the business of processing, dying, and selling flax, we can better understand why a scarlet thread from her window would have gone unnoticed. When we consider Rahab's enterprising abilities, the location of her house, and the traffic she attracted from travelers of the region, we recognize her as a political insider with a rich understanding of everything that was happening in Jericho and beyond.

Rahab's discussion with the spies showed that her concern was not for herself alone. Rahab loved her kin. She negotiated with the spies for "kindness unto my father's house" (Josh 2:12). The shrewdness of Rahab as a business woman was evident in her negotiations for the lives of her family members. She started by making the spies beholden to her. She hid them, redirected the king's men, gave the spies valuable information about the people of Jericho, and then instructed the Israelites for a safe return. Rahab realized that death for her city and its inhabitants was inevitable. She expected the devastation of the war to be total. Despite the expected siege, Rahab believed God could deliver her, and she was equally certain He would save her family.

Canaan and Jericho

Rahab was a Canaanite. That identifier does not specify her nation or tribe of origin. The name "Canaanite" was used to denote all non-Israelite people in the land conquered under Joshua. Canaanite has also been used to identify land areas and cultural practices. Some people have related the term to Ham, the son of Noah, and thus to the curse pronounced in Gen 9:22-25. (Erroneously, the curse has been used to justify the enslavement of people of African descent.) Because the name Canaanite has varied contexts and definitions, we can only be certain that Rahab was not an Israelite.

Rahab lived in Jericho, a city that provided access to trade routes, mountains, and the other cities of Canaan. Jericho was one of the fortified, or walled, cities of the Canaanite region. In fact, the walls of Jericho were its chief characteristic and the protection for the city's inhabitants. It is believed the Jericho wall actually comprised several walls. The first was a stabilizing stone wall about 15 feet in height. Resting above this structure was a free-standing retaining wall made of mud. It was six feet thick and stood 18 to 24 feet high. Another wall sat atop the retaining wall.[5] While the heights of the walls do not seem impressive today, they were sufficient to deter would-be invaders. It was the walled cities that had frightened the spies Moses sent, causing them to believe there were giants in the land (Num 13:2, 26-29).

The walls of Jericho were so massive that they supported houses. Rahab lived in the walls of the city (Josh

2:15). According to archaeologists, there were houses in the Jericho site that "were situated between the upper and lower city walls... (and) the lower wall formed the back wall of the house." Such houses also had a window or opening as reported in the book of Joshua.[6] From her house, Rahab had full access to the entrance of the walls and full view of what was happening inside and outside the city.

The Invasion

The welcome the spies received in Jericho is proof that while Moses and the Israelite people were in the wilderness for forty years their presence did not go unnoticed. Egypt was a superpower. The Canaanites were aware that the God of Israel was with the former slaves when they left Egypt. They understood that the battle had been between the God of Israel and the plethora of gods, including Pharaoh, who were declared to be on Egypt's side.

After the report of the returning spies, Israel moved to Shittim, where Joshua reiterated the instructions for the invasion (Josh 3:1). Then the host of Israel prepared for battle through a series of worship practices that included sanctification, circumcision, creating a memorial, and observing the Passover. These acts reiterated the covenant relationship and confirmed God's provision and deliverance. Fortified by their God and encouraged through their preparation, the Israelites were prepared to take the land.

Jericho was accustomed to war. The attack by Israel, however, was very different. As the Hebrew army marched around the walls of Jericho, there must have been fear and confusion inside the walls. The warriors of Jericho were trapped inside their city by an army that did not attack. The king and his advisers must have wondered what the invaders' strategy was. We can only imagine the turmoil that went on inside the walls of the city and the houses of Jericho's citizens. The king and the people of Jericho realized the God of the Host of Israel was there to vanquish them, but this manner of warfare was unknown. The trumpet sound signaled victory even before the battle began. The triumphant march around the walls with the ark of the Lord was inexplicable. The intimidation of these actions day after day would have created a psychological warfare like none they had experienced. Jericho was accustomed to war, and Rahab was expecting deliverance, but she, too, must have wondered what God was about to do.

GOD IN HER LIFE

It seems unlikely that we would have something to say about God in Rahab's life, particularly if we insist on defining her by the title "harlot." It is probably fair to say she was a polytheist. She lived in Canaan and was familiar with the many gods worshiped by her people and the surrounding nations. Basically, there were no atheists in any of the non-Israelite nations described in the Bible. Everyone believed in and worshiped some god—if not several gods. Rahab saw the issue of the spies and the pending invasion not as an issue of human conquest but as a holy war that would reveal the power of the God of Israel.

Rahab's Confession of Faith

When Rahab met the spies, she confessed, "I know that

the Lord has given you this land" (Josh 2:9). She may have initially negotiated with the spies out of concern for the preservation of her family and her own life, but her confession is our first hint that her loyalties had shifted from the pagan gods of Canaan to the one true God of Israel. In revealing what she knew of God's encounter with Egypt forty years earlier, Rahab acknowledged what God was capable of doing and disclosed her confidence that He would do it again. Rahab was not "hedging her bets" or being opportunistic. The fact she is mentioned in the New Testament books of Hebrews and James confirms that Rahab's faith was genuine. This non-Israelite woman was fully convinced that Jehovah was the only God.

Rahab's Faith in Action

Despite her wealth and connections, Rahab realized that only God could save her and preserve her father's house. At risk of death from the king of Jericho, Rahab vowed to wait on the Lord. She essentially demonstrated the same faith the children of Israel had when they participated in the first Passover in preparation for their deliverance from Pharaoh (Exodus 12:11). When the death angel passed through Egypt, the Israelites were identified and saved because they placed the blood of the sacrifice over the doorposts. In similar fashion, when death and destruction come to Jericho, the Lord of Hosts would recognize the scarlet thread and spare Rahab and her family. Without knowing what was happening on the other side of the River, Rahab was prepared to obediently follow God. When the invasion began neither Rahab nor her loved ones left the house. They did not venture into the street or the byway. No matter how inexplicable the actions of Israel seemed, she did not panic. She and her family remained vigilant and believed that they would not be forsaken.

In the end, Rahab's actions months earlier led to the salvation of "her father, and her mother, and her brethren, and all that she had." As promised, the Israelites "brought out all her kindred, and left them without the camp of Israel" (Josh 6:23). A curse was put upon the city, but a vow had been made that "only Rahab the harlot shall live, she and all that are with her in the house, because she hid the messengers that we sent" (v. 17). The city of Jericho was burned but Rahab and her "father's household" lived safely in Israel "unto this day" (v. 25).

Rahab, the Prophet

Tikva Frymer-Kensky calls Rahab a prophet of the Lord.[7] Rahab was the outsider who spoke truth when God commanded it to be spoken. Her words were the encouragement and confirmation the army needed to move forward in the conquest. Her declaration that Jericho was in fear of Israel was a prophetic utterance that declared who God was and the immensity of His power. It was Rahab who declared victory when she spoke to the men she protected on her roof. As a prophet of God, even before she knew His name, Rahab protected the name of the Lord and the people of God from the harm the king had in mind. Rahab, the prophet, realized that the ensuing battle between Israel and Jericho was a holy war. She knew that God would defeat the false gods and deliver the land into the hands of His people. Rahab is revered throughout the Bible because her prophetic voice issued a clear call to faith in a critical time, and her prophetic words still confirm the necessity of true faith.

WHAT HER LIFE SPEAKS

Rahab was not the typical woman of her day. She likely owned more than one business and was able to speak freely and confidently to the men who were in power including the king and his representatives (Josh 2:4-5). She achieved wealth and was a person who could get things done. She lived in a place of prominence and operated from a position of powerful independence. Because she is a heroine of faith and a champion of women's abilities, Rahab speaks to our natural and spiritual perspectives. The life she lived provides a rich tapestry from which women today can gain strength and confidence.

Concept 1: We Can Get Beyond the Burden of Reputation

When Jesus went to his hometown of Nazareth, he was ridiculed and rejected (Matt 13:53-58). He later asked the disciples, "Whom do men say that I the Son of man am?" (Matt 16:13). This was a reference to reputation. Jesus knew that the people did not understand what His presence and power meant. Despite what the people were saying, Jesus asked, "But whom say ye that I am" (Matthew 16:15)? This posed a question of character and relationship. Jesus was telling the disciples not to be swayed by public opinion. Their understanding of Jesus and later of themselves (and those who would become followers of Christ) must be based on the character of the person and their relationship to God. Jesus' words confirm that we cannot set a value upon our lives based on what other people arbitrarily say or think. Our lives and our confidence must be in the Lord and who He is enabling us to become through our relationship with Him.

Every honest Christian realizes that we have all failed to always do the right thing: "We have all sinned and come short of the glory of God" (Rom 3:23). We have made mistakes, and we have regrets. When we accept Christ as Lord and Savior, we are delivered from the burden of our pasts. "God freely and graciously declares that we are righteous. He did this through Christ Jesus when he freed us from the penalty for our sins" (Rom 3:24 NLT). This doesn't make us perfect. As John wrote to the church, "If we say that we have no sin, we deceive ourselves, and the truth is not in us. If we confess our sins, he is faithful and just to forgive us our sins, and to cleanse us from all unrighteousness" (1 John 1:8-9). Trusting in Christ gives us an advocate who "is even at the right hand of God, who also maketh intercession for us" (Rom 8:34). Having faith in Christ prepares us to take the focus off our past and place it on our hope in God. Salvation allows us to see our lives in light of God's call and choice of us (2 Pet 1:10). We cannot control what others say or think, but we can believe what God says and does.

Rahab trusted God, and her faith gave her a new perspective. While the people of Jericho waited in fear, Rahab stood fearlessly for God even in the face of the king's threats. While she awaited the return of the spies, she held tight to the promise of God's deliverance. While chaos, gossip, and worry gripped her neighbors, Rahab remained firm in her determination to gather her family as instructed. When the walls of Jericho fell, Rahab and her family were safely delivered. As the inhabitants of Jericho scattered and met their deaths, Rahab and her family entered into their promised deliverance. Although the city lay in terror, Rahab and her family lived in anticipation of their liberation. Like Rahab, we can overcome our past. We can turn our backs on shame, sorrow, and despair. We can live victoriously because we can trust God to deliver us each day and to give us His eternal peace.

Concept 2: We Must Wait On God

The spies were gone for a long time. It took three days for them to return to Joshua. It took time to walk from Shittim to the Jordan with all of the people and all of their possessions. It took months to complete the ritual preparations for battle and to celebrate the Passover. It took a while to go through the Jordan River and build the memorial. It even took seven days of walking around the city before the Lord brought down the walls. It would not be far-fetched to think that Rahab could have become anxious.

We can imagine that Rahab might have posed many questions in her mind: "What if those were not the *right* spies?" "What if they were killed by wild animals or some Canaanite in the hills?" "What if the dangerous trip had been too much for them?" Her heart might have grown fearful wondering if the men would keep their promise. "What if their leader disagreed?" "What if their God didn't want to save *any* Canaanites from His wrath?" The actions of others might have clouded Rahab's thinking. She may have wondered if her family would listen and be obedient. She may have been concerned that the king would hear what she was planning and issue a decree seeking to kill her. When the resolution did not come quickly, Rahab (like us) may have doubted God's response and questioned her own understanding.

We all have testimonies about a time when we *thought* God didn't hear us. We know of times when we prayed that God would heal a loved one or that some economic disaster would not occur. Although we may have waited patiently, it either did not happen or it happened much later or much differently from what we expected. The truth is that despite our hope, our faith can waver. Our humanity causes us to become impatient even with God. We realize that we have not always been faithful in our lives. We know in our hearts that we have failed someone along the way. We have even failed God! It seems natural, given our shortcomings, to fear that perhaps God won't hear or won't answer. We look at our sin and our shortfalls and wonder if God will be gracious unto us despite our failure toward Him.

There is a reason the Bible is replete with verses that tell us to wait on the Lord. Impatience, doubt, anxiety are human emotions. If we give in to them, we can lapse into depression or angrily lash out at others. We know such feelings and actions are wrong in the eyes of God and pointless in the world of man. What should we do then? A chorus often sung in prayer meetings reminds us to, "Keep on believing. God will answer prayer."

We pray because we trust in God, but we must also exercise our faith in order to strengthen our grip on "God's unchanging hand." We must not waver in our assurance that God will not fail. We must learn to discipline our spirits and minds so that we can hear what God is saying to our hearts. When we make Bible study part of our daily lives, we are training our minds to be patient in the Lord. When we make a point of praying daily, we are disciplining ourselves to hope in the Lord. When we begin to consider what God would have us do rather than what our friends, our societal norms, or even our own egos tell us, we are learning to wait patiently on the Lord with confidence that His Will is best for us.

Concept 3: We Must Be Bold in Seeking God's Favor
We must appreciate the boldness it took Rahab to exact a promise from the spies. She owned the house and had a reputation for doing what she wanted, but hiding the men who had come to find a way to destroy her city and kill all the people in it crossed the line. Nevertheless, Rahab boldly hid the men despite the threat by the king and his guards. She articulated the fear others in her city had probably only dared to whisper. "Your terror is fallen upon us ... all the inhabitants of the land faint because of you.... Our hearts did melt, neither did there remain any more courage in any man, because of you." (Josh 2:9, 11). She then confidently confronted the spies with a proposal that showed she had thought the matter through. "Now therefore, I pray you, swear unto me by (your) Lord..."
Rahab was so bold that she got beyond her own issues to think of others. She could have just said, "Remember me." Instead, she asked that her entire family be saved. Rahab gave specifics because she was a negotiator and understood contracts. She wanted to make her request crys-

tal clear. She asked the men to show "kindness unto my father's house… save alive my father, and my mother, and my brethren, and my sisters… and deliver our lives from death." This statement means more than the family of four! First, she asked for "her father's house." This phrase refers to her father and his entire household—wives, concubines, slaves, and servants. It refers to the children born into the family by the father, by his children, and by his servants. In addition to identifying the relationship she had to these people, she added a catch phrase: "and all they have." Whoever was in the house, whoever came to the place of salvation, Rahab wanted counted. Rahab was also specific about the condition she wanted for deliverance. She did not want them maimed or hurt. She was not saying "half-dead is better than all-dead." Rahab said, "Save alive" and "Deliver our lives from death."

Rahab's boldness was neither rash nor forward. It came from her assurance of who the God of Israel was. Her assurance did not come from having experienced the power of God in her life. She did not gain confidence to seek favor because of a past experience of a neighbor or a friend. Rahab's faith came strictly by hearing: "For we have heard how the LORD dried up the water of the Red Sea for you" (Josh 2:10). Her understanding of God's power was based on her hearing of His deliverance. Rahab realized that the Red Sea had not only opened, but the children of Israel had walked across this treacherous water—on the sea floor. She knew that not only was Israel saved, but also their enemies were destroyed when Pharaoh and his army ventured into the sea and were drowned. This miracle was so massive that the visualization of it put fear in the hearts of men hundreds of miles away and for generations that were not even born at the time of the escape.

We are encouraged by Rahab's faith because the boldness of her understanding exemplifies the description of faith in Romans 10:10-14, 17:

> [10]For with the heart man believeth unto righteousness; and with the mouth confession is made unto salvation.
> [11]For the scripture saith, Whosoever believeth on him shall not be ashamed.
> [12]For there is no difference between the Jew and the Greek: for the same Lord over all is rich unto all that call upon him.
> [13]For whosoever shall call upon the name of the Lord shall be saved.
> [14]How then shall they call on him in whom they have not believed? and how shall they believe in him of whom they have not heard? and how shall they hear without a preacher?...
> [17]So then faith cometh by hearing, and hearing by the word of God.

Rahab believed in her heart, and with her mouth she confessed that God could deliver her. She believed on the Lord and was not ashamed. She was an outsider from the faith of Israel, but she was convinced that God would not reject her based on her nationality or her country of origin. She believed in her heart that if she called on the God of Israel, if she spoke up regarding her faith in Him, God would show mercy toward her and her family. Rahab called on the Lord because she believed. She believed on God because she had heard. She had heard of God because the messengers of old had told the stories of the Red Sea. The men who came to her house were proof of all she had heard. Rahab was able to speak boldly and to prophesy regarding the victory the Lord would bring because God enabled her to do so. We do not know how many people were in Jericho or how many people were in her family. We only know that God had a word for Rahab to speak and that she boldly proclaimed who Jehovah was and what He would do because her faith was anchored in what she had heard about His mighty power.

Despite the words that are spoken against Rahab or the names that she is called even now, her message of the Good News of deliverance rings wonderfully in our ears. The encounter of Rahab and the spies reminds us that deliverance is ours. Her actions call our attention to how God is moving in our lives and throughout our communities. There may be bad things happening around us. We may live with the horrors of violence and in fear of personal, political, economic, and social disaster but Rahab's life has brought a message of hope and deliverance. All we have to do is believe the report. We can be bold in asking God for our salvation and the salvation of our families, our communities, and our world. We have heard the words of Rahab, and we know her message is from God.

Hearing Rahab

WHAT YOUR LIFE SPEAKS

Speak Your Truth

1. Rahab had to put fear aside in order to receive what she needed from God. What must you "put aside" in order to seek God's deliverance in your life?

2. What issues or negative perceptions hinder your actions or stymy your thinking?

Focus Your Faith

1. This discussion describes faith according to Romans 10. Review this passage and identify the phrases that give you the most encouragement.

2. This discussion has posed questions about what makes our faith wane. What has caused you to doubt or lose faith on occasion? How did you behave or think during those times? What strengthened your faith in those times?

USING YOUR VOICE

Ponder

1. Rahab's reputation has painted her in a negative light? When, if ever, have you allowed "reputation" or innuendo to taint your thinking about someone?

2. Consider your reputation. In what way is it reflective of how others see you? Do you agree that who they "see" is who you are? How do the expectations of others impact your self-esteem?

3. Rahab's knowledge of God relied heavily on what she had heard. Hearing is an important aspect of building faith. What do you "listen to" as part of your devotion?

Pray

1. Like most people, Rahab was concerned about her family. Create a prayer list of the members of your natural and spiritual family who are in need of extra attention and prayer.
2. Have a time of prayer when you ask God for or thank God for a special time of courage in your life or the life of a loved one.
3. Include in your prayers the people who are being affected by wars, natural disasters, street violence, terrorist acts, and other societal situations. Ask God to reveal how you can help.

Practice

1. Share your testimony with someone who does not know Christ as Savior.
2. Join a reputable group of Christians or community leaders to help make a change in a situation or the life of someone in your community.
3. Research a community, national, or global organization or ministry that you can support in their efforts to help people in need. Then follow through with a commitment.

Naomi

THE BOOK OF RUTH

HAVE YOU EVER KNOWN SOMEONE OF FAITH who seemed to have it all together? Did you secretly wonder how she made it without losing faith either in herself or God? Naomi was a person like that—a person who seemed to trust God even in the worst of times. For the rest of us, people like Naomi are intriguing. If we are honest, we admit that sometimes we think they can't be real. No one can take all of the pain and loss, and not be frustrated or angry. Where is their reality? What keeps them from breaking? Further, why can't we have that same resolve? As we follow Naomi's life, we find that she was frustrated, and she did get discouraged. We see her tears, and we hear her prayers. Most of all, we learn what she knew about God that helped her stay centered in the face of life and death.

SYNOPSIS

Naomi and her family moved to Moab because of a famine in Bethlehem-Judah. After relocating, Naomi's husband, Elimelech, died. Her sons, Mahlon and Chilion, later married (Ruth 1:4). For ten years, the two couples and Naomi lived together. When Mahlon and Chilion died, Naomi and her daughters-in-law, Ruth and Orpah, were left destitute in Moab.

When Naomi heard the famine was over in Bethlehem-Judah and that the people were enjoying God's bounty, she decided to return home. Because her daughters-in-law were young, she urged them to return to their mothers' houses where they would have the opportunity to remarry. Orpah agreed and returned home, but Ruth pleaded to go with Naomi. When the two women reached Bethlehem-Judah, Naomi was welcomed by old friends, but she was also overwhelmed by her grief. Naomi's name meant pleasant and was a reminder of her life as a younger woman. Because of the losses she had suffered, she asked her friends to call her Mara (bitterness) instead. While the famine was over in Judah, she and Ruth were poverty-stricken widows. One was a stranger to the community; the other was older and unable to garner the help they needed. Ruth realized something had to be done. She pleaded, "Let me go out into the harvest fields to pick up the stalks of grain left behind by anyone who is kind enough to let me do it" (Ruth 2:2 NLT). Naomi agreed.

Boaz was the owner of the field where Ruth gathered left-over wheat. She noticed his kindness in greeting his workers with a blessing when he came to check on the progress of the harvest. He also noticed a new woman among the gleaners. He inquired about her. He was told who Ruth was and remembered what he had heard about her kindness to Naomi. He ordered the workers to give Ruth extra grain, and he personally made sure she had food and drink while she worked. When Ruth returned home she told Naomi of the kindness of the field's owner and showed her the bounty she had been given.

Ruth did not know who Boaz was, but Naomi did. He was a distant kinsman of her husband, Elimelech. Naomi immediately recognized Boaz's kindness to Ruth as more than casual. His generosity continued through the harvest season and confirmed that he was willing to take care of Ruth and Naomi. This meant that Boaz could be the one to redeem Elimelech's property and provide a new life for Ruth. With this hope, Naomi sent Ruth to meet Boaz at the threshing floor where, according to custom, the young woman would request that Boaz serve as the provider and protector for her and Naomi.

Boaz eagerly accepted; however, there was a legal obstacle to this arrangement. Undaunted, Boaz began the process for restoration. He called a meeting with the elders and the nearest kinsman and explained what had to be done. His persuasive case resulted in his gaining the right to restore Naomi's property and marry Ruth. The child that was born from their marriage carried the name of Ruth's deceased husband, Mahlon, Naomi's son. Thus Naomi and Elimelech's family lineage was redeemed through this child who would become the grandfather of King David.

LIFE IN HER WORLD

Elimelech's decision to leave Judah during the famine took

the entire family into another country. Upon first glance, it seems logical to move in search of a better life in a more prosperous country, but the decision to go to Moab was much more complicated than we might think.

Moab and the Moabites

Moab was an idolatrous nation. Its people were descendants of Lot, Abraham's nephew. Lot's son, Moab, was born out of an incestuous relationship between Lot and his daughter (Gen 19:30-36). The Moabites were polytheists, and their national god was Chemosh.[1] They were also known to practice human sacrifice (2 Kings 3:27). Like the Canaanites, the Amalekites, and the Philistines, the Moabites are listed among the enemies of Israel. They are among the tribes that God told Israel to destroy during the conquest under Joshua.

The ongoing hostilities led to several injunctions against Moab by God. Nevertheless, the histories of the two nations were intertwined. During the wilderness journey, Israel was forbidden to camp inside Moab. Instead, they made camp in the plains of Moab just outside Jericho (Num 22:1). It was in the plains of Moab that Moses told the tribes which parcels of land each would inherit. This was also the place of Israel's last encampment before entering the Promised Land (Joshua 13:32). While the book of Ruth takes place during the time of the judges, the ties between Moab and Israel continued into the period of the kings and the prophets. For example, David had a Moabite warrior as a "mighty man" in his army (1 Chr 11:46). King Solomon married a Moabite woman and built "a high place" outside Jerusalem for her to worship Chemosh, their chief god (1 Kings 11:7-9).

When Elimelech and Naomi entered Moab, they became strange worshipers in a land filled with idolaters. At the time of the famine, Moab had the food, but the centuries of hatred and the differences in culture would have made the decision to go there a difficult one. The move took Naomi and her family to people who either did not know or resented the God of Israel. For Israelite men, Moab was not a desirable place to find a wife. The Israelites preferred marriage within the clan so that tribal heritage and the worship of Jehovah-God would continue. Naomi's sons, however, were not in a position to marry women from Hebrew homes. They had to select wives from the pagan women around them. After their deaths, these Moabite women, Ruth and Orpah, remained faithful to their Israelite mother-in-law, Naomi.

A Widow's Dilemma

News of the blessing in Judah implies that the Lord was not blessing in Moab. Naomi had gone to Moab in search of food. Now she would return from Moab for the same reason. Before the famine, life in Bethlehem-Judah had been good. She recalled the parcel of land she and Elimelech had owned. She remembered the friends and relatives they left behind. Naomi may have thought her experience would be the same as when she left, but her status as a widow would make life perilous. While married women were under the protection of their husbands, widows were expected to be cared for by their male children or other men in their families who would be responsible for them. Even if they had no family, the Law made provisions for widows. If a widow was in debt, her cloak could not be taken as security (Deut 24:17). Like strangers and the Levites who had no land of their own, widows were to be permitted to eat from the bounty of the land (Deut 14:29; 24:19-21). The Law allowed for widows, Levites, and strangers to glean in the fields at harvest time (Lev 23:22). Women had no judicial rights, but the Law maintained, "Cursed is anyone who denies justice to foreigners, orphans, or widows"(Deut 27:19).

In addition to the death of her husband and sons, Naomi had also suffered the loss of property in Judah. In order to retrieve the land, Naomi needed to have her husband's closest male relative act on her behalf. After Ruth's encounter with Boaz, Naomi hoped he would represent her. But the issue of Naomi's land is unclear. Was Naomi selling the land or buying it back? There are two possible explanations. Naomi may have owned the land but was forced to sell it because of her dire poverty. Another explanation is that Elimelech sold the land before going to Moab. Because land in Israel belonged to God and could not be sold permanently, Naomi had the right to buy it back. In this option, she was selling her right to buy back the land to another family member. Thus Naomi was asking a kinsman to purchase back the land, keep it in the family, and provide the financial support she needed.[2]

In stark contrast to any possible expectations, reality came into focus as Naomi entered the city of Bethlehem-Judah. "I left full," she cried, "But I have returned empty… the Almighty has afflicted me?" (Ruth 1:20-21 NKJV). Naomi's confession to the women of Judah was not anti-God. It was simply a statement of fact and the basis for the theological quandary Naomi faced. The Israelites looked at everything as either a blessing or a curse from God. As a foreigner in Moab, Naomi saw the God of Israel as both the One who left her in despair and the only Deliverer available. Naomi realized she had no prospects in Moab, but she had hope in Judah. If she wanted to end her suffering, the widowed Naomi must return to Bethlehem. So despite all she had suffered, Naomi held on to her faith in God and made the journey to her homeland.

A Mother's Plea

Naomi was determined to return to Judah, but she wanted Orpah and Ruth to return to their mothers' houses. Naomi said, "mothers' houses" rather than "fathers' houses" because Hebrew mothers were influential in their homes. Naomi saw Moabite mothers in the same light. According to Dr. Leila Leah Bronner:

> The mother of the Bible is a figure of power. She influences the course of life in her home and, in some cases, wider society. The biblical mother is a force to be reckoned with in social, political and religious spheres. Her power stems in part from her role as wife, but far more so from the nurturing and influential relationship she has with her children. No other biblical woman, whether wife, sister or daughter, seems to enjoy the same status and power as the mother. As the mother of the Bible cares for her clan, she does so with wisdom and purpose, acquiring authority and position within the household and beyond.[3]

It was because of Naomi's influence as a mother that these young women refused to leave her. As the cultural conduit for her family, Naomi would have spent countless hours teaching Ruth and Orpah to care for the family and telling them of her love of God. Her conversations with them and her sons would have been filled with stories of life in Judah. But in making a case for the young women to return home, Naomi argued that they must face reality. She was destitute and not certain she had a relative who could take care of any of them. Sarcastically, Naomi says Ruth and Orpah could not wait on any babies she birthed to become old enough to marry. Naomi's outburst indicated her frustration. The pressure of their expectation was beyond her comprehension. We can almost hear her plea: "Don't ask any more of me. I have no more sons to give. Waiting on me and expecting me to provide an answer is too much. Go home. I am a mother without sons and without land. My husband, too, is gone. Your mothers can help you. Return to them." Naomi understood the plight of the foreigner and the cruel reality of life as a childless widow. She knew that in Judah, Ruth and Orpah would be destitute strangers as she had been in Moab.

Orpah understood the advice Naomi gave her. She returned to her mother's home. In essence, Orpah returned to a place of comfort and support. She returned to the hope she had in the beginning, the hope for a husband and children. In fact, she, like Naomi, saw the return to Moab as her only choice. Ruth, however, stayed with Naomi. She, too, had hope. Her hope was born from Naomi's faith in the God of Israel. Because of Naomi's faith, Ruth believed God would deliver them both. She believed

God's blessing upon Naomi would also be upon her. Ruth went to Judah because Naomi was the mother who gave her hope.

GOD IN HER LIFE

It is easy to say that Naomi's journey to Moab was an abandonment of her God to search for provision from other gods. That statement does not represent the influences on and experiences in Naomi's life. Neither does it hint at the fiber of her faith in God. Naomi's outburst in sending her daughters-in-law to their mothers spoke of her frustration with her circumstance and the pressure she felt each day. But like Job, Naomi never cursed God! She remembered all the times in her life when God had sustained her. Her memories gave her confidence that God would do that and more again.

God in Her Home

We know that for at least ten years after her sons married, Naomi lived in Moab with two women who came from pagan homes. While the people around her worshiped multiple gods, Naomi honored the Law of Moses: "Ye shall make you no idols nor graven image, neither rear you up a standing image, neither shall ye set up any image of stone in your land, to bow down unto it: for I am the LORD your God" (Lev 26:1). As a Hebrew mother, her home was shaped by her faith. Her worship and memories of family as well as her recounting God's blessings upon Israel taught her children about God. Naomi's decision to return to Judah is proof she never wavered from following God. She was not swayed by the pagan land where she lived, and she was unmoved by the claims of those who worshiped the idols of Moab.

In fact, Naomi's lifestyle was so different from that of the Moabites that it had an impact on her daughters-in-law. When Orpah left Naomi to return to her mother's house, Naomi declared that Orpah had "gone back unto her people, and unto her gods" (Ruth 1:15). Orpah returned from following Naomi's rules of worship and home life to worship in the idolatrous tradition of her family. In contrast, Ruth begged Naomi to allow her to go to Judah (Ruth 1:16). The rendering of these words in The Message Bible leaves no shadow in their meaning: "Don't force me to leave you; don't make me go home." With these words, Ruth renounced everything that was hers before she met Naomi—her land, her home, her family, and the gods of her childhood. As the mother of her household, Naomi used her power and influence to teach these young women who the God of Israel was, and Ruth learned the lessons well.

The Presence of *Hesed*

Because she was an Israelite and a worshiper of Jehovah, Naomi knew the meaning of *hesed*. This Old Testament theological term has a meaning in the Hebrew that cannot be adequately translated into English. Words such as mercy, faithfulness, loyalty, and goodness do not go deep enough in expressing *hesed*. When God passed before Moses in Exodus 34:6-7, the Almighty described Himself saying,

God! The LORD!
>   The God of compassion and mercy!
I am slow to anger
>   and filled with unfailing love and faithfulness.
I lavish unfailing love to a thousand generations.
>   I forgive iniquity, rebellion, and sin...

The New International Version reads: "the compassionate and gracious God, slow to anger, abounding in love and faithfulness." *Hesed* is translated in these texts as "love" and "faithfulness," but the word goes much deeper. In an effort to translate *hesed*, Bible versions differ in their word choices. The King James Version translates *hesed* as "abundant in goodness and truth."

We can identify God's *hesed* in His faithful love and favor. *Hesed* is more than just a feeling that God will care for those who belong to Him. God's *hesed* is the essence of His loyalty and His actions. *Hesed* is an understanding that God will provide for those who descended from Abraham. God's *hesed* had been shown to Abraham when he went into an unknown land. Even Abraham's unborn offspring were promised God's *hesed*, His provision and blessing. It was God's *hesed* that gave Isaac to an old and barren couple with the promise of offspring that would be as numerous as the stars. Naomi depended on God's *hesed*. She knew God's *hesed* had taken Jacob's son, Joseph, to Egypt so that in the time of famine, Isaac's family would be helped. The *hesed* of the Lord called Moses into a far country to prepare him to deliver Israel from Pharoah's hand and to give the Law that would teach the nation to worship the Lawgiver "with all thine heart, and with all thy soul, and with all thy might" (Deut 6:5). It was the Lord's *hesed* that gave Naomi hope.

One problem for the non-Hebrew reader is that *hesed* is wholly God's but not only God's. *Hesed* occurs between two parties—either God and humans or between two persons. *Hesed* is the essence of community and the reflection of God's abundant grace to those He chooses. Iain Duguid points out in an article entitled "Loyal-Love" that the *hesed* God demands of humans is the "love and service that we owe to the other person simply because he is part of the covenant community."[4] Micah 6:8 states, "He hath shewed thee, O man, what is good; and what doth the LORD require of thee, but to do justly, and to love mercy, and to walk humbly with thy God?" This is a call to *hesed*. God has shown His *hesed* and expects humans to show *hesed* to others. While the verse uses "mercy" to mean *hesed*, the entire sentence undergirds the need for and outpouring of *hesed* in human relationships and acts of justice. Naomi experienced this in both Moab and Judah.

God's *Hesed* in Moab – Naomi's journey to Moab with Elimelech cannot be seen as a mistake. Rather, it must be seen as God's *hesed* because God provided for her when her storehouse was empty in Judah. It was God's *hesed* that took them safely to Moab and that kept them faithfully while they were there. Her family had grown in Moab. While her sons had no children, they had taken wives. It was God's *hesed* that positioned these young women to care for Naomi when she had no one else. It was God's *hesed* that sent word to Naomi that Judah was prospering.

Her hope was restored when she realized that she had a place to go that would welcome her as family. She would no longer be a stranger in a strange land. It was God's *hesed* that prepared her for the journey and took her safely to Judah, where she could see for herself the blessings of the Lord.

God's *Hesed* in Bethlehem-Judah – When Ruth and Naomi arrived in Judah God's *hesed* opened the door for the restoration Naomi sought. Ruth had no idea what field she should glean, but she was directed by the Lord to the place He had prepared for her. Ruth had no idea why Boaz was so gracious to her, but Naomi realized that in God's *hesed*, Boaz's field was the correct place to receive favor. Because of God's *hesed*, His covenant people are expected to provide *hesed* to others. When Boaz was told who Ruth was, he recognized her actions as a blessing (*hesed*) upon her mother-in-law and a sign of God's provision for the older woman. *Hesed* was demonstrated when Boaz served as the near kinsman who redeemed the land and married Ruth.

God's *Hesed* Extends to Each Generation — Children are the continuation of lineage. It is through the children that parents and ancestors are remembered. Naomi thought she had lost everything including a future memory of her husband and his family because her sons died childless. The birth of Obed, the son of Ruth and Boaz, redeemed all that Naomi had lost. When Obed was born, he was placed on Naomi's bosom (Ruth 4:16). In Ruth 4:14-15, the women sang:

> Blessed be the LORD, which hath not left thee this day without a kinsman, that his name may be famous in Israel. And he shall be unto thee a restorer of thy life, and a nourisher of thine old age: for thy daughter in law, which loveth thee, which is better to thee than seven sons, hath born him…

Ruth bore the child, and Naomi continued to operate as the Hebrew mother to the next generation of her family. She would share with this child her faith in God, her love of Judah, and the stories of God's *hesed* in the life of their family knowing that God's *hesed* would be with the child always.

WHAT HER LIFE SPEAKS

To most Christians today, Naomi was a good mother and wife who influenced her daughter-in-law's life and remarriage to Boaz. Naomi's life, however, speaks more than that.

Concept 1: Faith Is Our Core

The NIV Bible calls faith the "confidence in what we hope for and assurance about what we do not see" (Hebrews 11:1). Naomi had faith. From the human standpoint, she could not have foreseen that her husband and sons would die. After their deaths, the darkness surrounding her life could have become her focal point and wedded her to despair. Even after she and her daughters-in-law left their home and started to make their way out of Moab, she stopped and re-thought the idea (Ruth 1:7). We cannot know what made Naomi reconsider the trip or ask the young women if they were really committed to it, but her hesitation could have turned into a reason not to continue. It did for Orpah.

But Naomi understood God as Deliverer. That was the basis of her faith and the foundation on which she built a new life. Naomi grew up hearing how God delivered her ancestors from Egypt and took them to the Promised Land. Her family had no doubt practiced the rituals of faith as described in the books of the Pentateuch. From Naomi's life, we learn that if we value the biblical account of God's deliverance, we can develop the confidence that He will deliver us. Faith is our response to the mercy and grace God bestows upon us. "Without faith it is impossible to please him: for he that cometh to God must believe that he is, and that he is a rewarder of them that diligently seek him" (Hebrews 11:6). God rewards our faith with greater faith because he grants us more mercy and more grace—to see us through the situations that comprise our lives.

Even when we face the pain of death and the scourge of loneliness, with faith we can move forward and not give in to the temptation to give up. If we take a step backward or get weary from what life brings into our families, our jobs, our communities, or our nation, we can still hold onto our faith. With faith we can sustain the hope to move beyond our circumstance and to learn from it. We cannot lament the past forever, and we cannot continue to blame the events or the people who failed us. Instead, we must strengthen our faith in the God who delivers because faith is the core of all we do. Faith identified Naomi as a worshiper of God. Our faith identifies us as Christians.

Concept 2: The Way We Live Matters

Naomi lived in a society where she may not have connected very well with those around her. The rules of conduct and engagement, especially along religious lines, were much different from her tradition. But what difference did it make if she connected or not? Who would have known if she had decided not to worship God or even to worship the Moabite gods? Who would have known if she had taken off in the night and left her daughters-in-law to fend for themselves? After all, once she got to Judah, she would be back in her own circle. In Judah, there would be no witnesses of what she did in Moab.

The truth is that God and Naomi would have known. Naomi realized that how she lived was a matter of integrity and character. Both of these qualities have been described as the things we do when we think no one is watching. Naomi stayed true to herself and to God because she knew that, at all times, someone is watching; and, even if no human is watching, God is. Naomi did not live the life of an Israelite worshiper because her daughters-in-law were watching. She was not trying to prove anything or make a point to her neighbors. Instead, Naomi made her relationship with God the impetus for her living. His Law was her foundation. His promises were her hope. His history of deliverance assured her liberation no matter when or how disaster struck. It did not matter if anyone was watching.

What did matter was that Naomi was able to honestly embrace God as her own and be true to the person He was calling her to be. Naomi had no idea Ruth would journey to Judah with her, marry a Israelite man, and give birth to a child who would continue the legacy of Elimelech—but God knew! Had Naomi not grasped the truth of integrity and character as the hallmarks of her faith, she would not have been a central figure in the ancestry of King David—the future offspring of Ruth's child.

Like Naomi, we can never really know how God's plan will unfold. We may never know whose life is influenced by our faith. We may not realize how powerful our witness is to others. We do not know how our walk influences our families and friends who, without our knowing it, are watching to see if our faith is real and our testimony valid. We never know what door our actions will open or close. We cannot know what the future holds. Because we cannot know these things, we must live each day knowing that how we live matters in God's plan for us.

Concept 3: Our Trials Are Not the End Game

In response to his wife's suggestion that he curse God and die, Job answered, "What? Shall we receive good at the hand of God, and shall we not receive evil?" (Job 2:10). This was probably Naomi's thought when she considered all that had happened to her in Moab. Despite our faith in God, life happens. Loved ones die, financial security fails, natural disasters strike, and we can always expect the unexpected. As Jesus pointed out in the Sermon on the Mount (Matt 5), the Father "maketh his sun to rise on the evil and on the good, and sendeth rain on the just and on the unjust." Being a Christian does not negate the bad stuff. It does, however, give us a different perspective. When life is overwhelming, we may find ourselves in the throes of complaint and despair. But if we only consider life from the perspective of what has befallen us and what we have lost, we will lose hope.

Naomi's life tells us that there is another way to look at our circumstances. The New Testament confirms this. If we expand our view to consider our problems from the perspective of James 1:3, then we realize that "the trying of your faith worketh patience." The New Living Translation renders James 1:3 as "when your faith is tested, your endurance has a chance to grow." There is a greater purpose and a positive outcome to all we face. Like strength training, if we never increase the weights, we will never increase our muscle mass or stamina. If we give up at the first sign of trouble or let anguish overtake us early in our Christian walk, we will not enjoy the benefits of our faith journey. Our witness will be weak. Our ability to remain strong in a crisis or to help others navigate the vicissitudes of life will be lost. Naomi's statement to the women of Israel regarding the hardness of life in Moab reminds us that our trials increase our patience. If we make it through one trial, we will be better able to handle the next one. Trials will come, problems will occur, but through it all, we will be "mature and complete, not lacking" (James 1:4, NIV). The trial is not the end game; victory is!

Concept 4: We Must Remember *Hesed*

Remembering the Lord's *hesed* is a spiritual discipline that toughens us emotionally and mentally. Jeremiah wrote that God's mercies and compassion are new every morning (Lam 3:22-23). Like Naomi, each day we must expect that God's hand will be in our lives. Every day will not be joyful. Neither can we expect everything to go our way.

We can, however, expect God to provide an outcome that will protect us and provide for us while we face the challenges, tragedies, and triumphs of life. Bad things do happen to good people, but God's hand preserves the souls of His people in the midst of bad things. That is the presence and power of God's *hesed*.

Hesed is the basis of community and is expected to flow, not just from God, but from person to person. Knowing and experiencing God's *hesed* demands we show grace and mercy to those around us. That must be the hallmark of our Christian community of faith. We must resist the tendency of our society to either, "Do unto others *before* they do unto you," or to "Do unto others *because* they have done unto you." Getting even, getting back, and getting ahead cannot characterize our lives. Our lives must reflect what God has provided for us. We show kindness because God is good to us. We show mercy because Jesus paid for our sins and we received mercy from God. We give graciously unto others in tangible and intangible ways because God has graciously poured His love upon us. With His loving kindness He has drawn us (Jer 31:3). God's *hesed,* His grace and mercy, are active in our lives so that our extension of grace and mercy to others will draw them to the Lord. In all we do and are, we must remember the importance of *hesed.* Remembering God's *hesed* becomes the discipline that enables us to practice *hesed* in our lives and relationships.

Hearing Naomi

WHAT YOUR LIFE SPEAKS

Speak Your Truth

1. Despite difficulty of Naomi's journey, she was able to maintain hope in God's deliverance. What helps you maintain hope?

2. Naomi's integrity characterized how she lived. What characterizes your life? Are you pleased with that characterization? Is God?

Focus Your Faith

1. This discussion identified a number of Scriptures that describe God's *hesed*. Select several to reflect on during your daily devotion.

2. How does the realization of God's *hesed* speak to your life?

3. In what ways do you demonstrate God's *hesed* in your life? Is that sufficient?

USING YOUR VOICE

Ponder

1. Scholars say that *hesed* cannot be adequately defined in English. Despite that, what characteristics of God do you see as indications of His *hesed*?

2. This discussion quoted Lamentations 3:22-23: "It is of the Lord's mercies that we are not consumed, because his compassions fail not. They are new every morning:

great is thy faithfulness." What new mercies and compassions of the Lord are you grateful for today?

Pray

1. Pray for a greater appreciation of God's *hesed* in your life.
2. Ask the Lord to help you show hospitality to others in new and deeper ways.

Practice

1. There are people in our communities, cities, and towns that are facing plights similar to Naomi's: despair, homelessness, loneliness, dire poverty, and more. Organize a group to help by supporting an organization that addresses one or more of these issues. You might consider an auxiliary or group in your church, the Salvation Army, the Red Cross, or a local agency.
2. There are communities in every state of this country that are classified as "food deserts" because of the lack of affordable groceries and fresh produce. According to U.S. Department of Agriculture, 49.1 million people in this country lived in food-insecure households in 2013.
   - Volunteer to help in a food pantry or feeding program in your area or church.
   - Mobilize a prayer group to pray for those in need.
   - Organize an action team to find ways to address this need.

Ruth

THE BOOK OF RUTH

WHAT DO THESE FILMS have in common?

Cooley High
The Breakfast Club
Rebel Without A Cause
Stand By Me

If you said they were all films about coming of age, you are right. In many ways, the book of Ruth is also about coming of age. As we listen to Ruth's life, we follow a trail filled with changing relationships, social realities, agricultural traditions, and religious customs. In the end, we recognize a young woman who comes of age as she learns the true meaning of faith in her journey to find God.

SYNOPSIS

Ruth was a Moabite. She married an Israelite refugee named Mahlon who had migrated to Moab with his family some years earlier when a famine devastated their homeland of Judah. Ruth's brother-in-law, Chilion, also married a Moabite woman. Her name was Orpah. After marriage, these women lived in the home of their husbands' family. It was common and necessary for the generations to live together for economic stability and family unity. Because of the earlier death of their father, the sons assumed responsibility for their mother, Naomi. But life in Moab was not easy. Within about ten years both sons died. The three women were left widowed, childless, and impoverished.

When Naomi heard that Judah was prosperous, she decided to return to her native land. Her daughters-in-law started the journey with her, but Naomi decided it was best if she returned to Judah alone. She explained to the young women that they should remain in Moab, where they had families who would welcome them. Both Orpah and Ruth loved Naomi and initially resisted her suggestion. Eventually, and through tears, Orpah returned to her Moabite family with Naomi's blessing.

Ruth, however, was determined to go with Naomi. She realized Naomi would not make it alone —on the return journey or in Judah—unless someone took care of her. Naomi had been a mother to Ruth. Now Ruth would be a daughter to her. In pleading with Naomi to let her continue the trip, Ruth confessed, "Whither thou goest, I will go…" (Ruth 1:16). In contrast to her sister Orpah, who returned to the Moabite tribe, the resolute Ruth journeyed to Judah with Naomi.

Without animals and alone, the two women likely walked the long and treacherous journey from Moab to Bethlehem, a trip of more than 30 miles. They arrived in Bethlehem in the spring, at the height of the harvest season (Ruth 1:22). The possibilities for a better life seemed good to Ruth, but her first glance at Judah caused Naomi to remember all she and Elimelech had left behind years earlier. In the pain of loss, Naomi decided that Mara was a better name for her because of the bitterness she had experienced at the hand of God. Ruth did not speak during Naomi's agonizing declaration. She understood that they were in a desperate situation, but she had faith that the God Naomi served would provide a better life than what they had experienced in Moab. Undeterred, Ruth asked permission to glean from the field of anyone who would allow her, a stranger, to do so. Naomi agreed. Through divine providence, Ruth found herself in a field owned by a man named Boaz.

Ruth worked hard to gather enough grain for Naomi and herself. When Boaz came to check on the workers, he noticed the stranger among the women who had come to glean. His servants explained that Ruth was a foreigner, a Moabite woman. The community grapevine had already made Boaz aware of how gracious this foreigner had been to her mother-in-law. The arduous work of gathering leftover grain was proof Ruth had chosen to care for Naomi as her own mother. An impressed Boaz arranged for Ruth to be shown every kindness.

When Ruth returned home that evening, she told Naomi all that had happened. Boaz had invited Ruth to the table with the workers. He had offered her extra grain, more than enough for herself and Naomi. He even encouraged her to remain in his fields for the duration of the harvest season where he could see that she was safe. Naomi told Ruth to continue to glean in Boaz's fields because he was a wealthy relative (Ruth 2:22). Naomi understood that God was providing a way to restore the land she and Elimelech had previously owned. Through his generosity, Boaz was offering to be a provider and protector to the women. Over time, his actions also demonstrated that marriage to Ruth could be possible. With this hope, Naomi instructed Ruth to begin the proposal process (Ruth 3).

The concept of lying at a man's feet on a threshing floor as a proposal of marriage is lost to our modern understanding. With her actions, Ruth essentially asked Boaz to provide continued protection and provision for her and her mother, Naomi.[1] Her overture also indicated that she could provide Boaz, an older man, with offspring. Boaz recognized Ruth's offer of marriage and was elated she chose him rather than a younger man. Under Israelite custom, however, he could only marry Ruth and claim the land if he were the nearest kinsman. Boaz was not but he began the legal process of claiming the land and assuring he would be the one to marry Ruth. After Boaz's skillful negotiations and God's merciful hand, Ruth and Boaz married, and the land was redeemed. Their firstborn child restored Naomi's joy and eventually became the grandfather of King David.

LIFE IN HER WORLD

A widow without a means of support was considered to be as destitute as an orphaned child. Ruth was a young widow, and re-marriage for her would provide the help and protection she and Naomi needed. Despite her Moabite background, Ruth hoped for a better life and expected the blessings of God. But Ruth was also a foreigner and a Moabite, which made her prospects for marriage in Israel unlikely.

The Plight of a Stranger

The country of Moab worshiped "other gods," including Chemosh, the national god. During the time of Israel's Wilderness Journey and the Conquest of Canaan, Israelites were instructed to annihilate several nations, including Moab, because they were considered enemies of God. Israel failed to do so, and the warning against intermarriage was stern. "You must not intermarry with them. Do not let your daughters and sons marry their sons and daughters." The reason: "For they will lead your children away from me to worship other gods" (Deut 7:3, NLT). For ten years, Ruth (a Moabite) had been married to Naomi's son, Mahlon (an Israelite). The couple never had children. Ruth's only concern was to be a true daughter to her mother-in-law and worship the God of Israel. However, her decision to go with Naomi labeled as a childless and widowed stranger living in Judah.

In Hebrew, the stranger (Heb. *goi*) or sojourner (Heb. *ger*) from a foreign nation was not to be oppressed because God "ensures that orphans and widows receive justice, He shows love to the foreigners living among you and gives them food and clothing" (Deut 10:18 NLT). Impoverished sojourners were to receive the benefits due a poor person of Hebrew descent. God's grace toward the stranger or foreigner and the widow set the example for how Israel was to treat the unfortunate and poor among them. Leviticus 19:33 confirms, "Do not take advantage of foreigners who live among you in your land. Treat them like native-born Israelites, and love them as you love yourself. Remember that you were once foreigners living in the land of Egypt." (NLT).

The Harvest Season

Ruth and Naomi arrived in Bethlehem-Judah at the height of the barley season, which was the first crop in the harvest cycle.[2] When the harvest was ripe, the owner hired people to help gather the crops. In Israel, farmers were forbidden from stripping the fields completely; therefore, not every stalk was clean as the workers moved through the fields. The process of gathering the leftover or missed grain was called gleaning, a term that means to go over a "second time."[3] The Law dictated that widows, the poor, and the strangers could glean from the edges of the fields and gather from the stalks that were left behind (Deut 24:19-21). During the harvest season, many poor people, including women, gravitated to the fields where they were looked upon kindly or where there were adequate crops to gather. The workers were separated from the gleaners and had better accommodations including refreshments, water, and a place to rest from the sun. Boaz's offer of food, water, and extra grain for Ruth was extraordinary. His offer to keep her in his field so that his workers could protect her was proof of how difficult and dangerous it was for women to work the fields alone.

Harvesting included gathering and preparing the various crops for use. The harvest fields were adjacent to the processing areas. Every field had a threshing floor. The threshing floor was a flat, circular outside area near the grain fields. So that harvesting of barley, wheat, and similar crops would be easier, the tools and animals used to separate and process each crop were kept in the same vicinity. The threshing floor was usually on a hill so that the wind could blow the unusable chaff as the crop was processed. The winepress and the vineyards were nearby so that those crops could be harvested and processed. Above the threshing floor stood the watchtower, which provided a shady spot where workers could be refreshed. Ruth's work in the fields was done near the threshing floor. Her proposal of marriage and overture to Boaz regarding his protection was made at night but not in a secluded spot. It is likely other workers slept there during the harvesting season because of the amount of work to be done (Ruth 2:23).[4]

The Feasts

While some ideas and events may have been familiar or similar to what Ruth experienced in her native land, other customs and traditions were new to her. For the Hebrew people, the seasons were marked by harvests and corresponded to three principle feasts of the Israelite faith: The Passover, the Feast of Weeks, and the Feast of Tabernacles (Deut. 16).[5]

The Passover

The Passover (Deut 16:1) commemorated God's deliverance of His people from the bondage of Egypt. At that time, the Israelites were poor, enslaved persons. The Law demanded that the Passover be observed in April during the barley harvest. Barley was a staple often available to the poor and used to feed livestock.[6] It was a reminder of the difficulties Israel faced in the land of the Pharaohs. While the King James translation refers to corn in Ruth 2:2, corn was not a crop in the Middle East. A better translation is "grain" (Heb. shibbol). Thus the people who worked in the barley fields ate parched grain and bread dipped in vinegar (Ruth 2:14).[7] Lentils and peas were among the other crops that were harvested in April during barley harvest time.

The Feast of Weeks

The scattered spring showers during and after the barley harvest helped increase wheat production. Wheat was the primary crop and was harvested in June.[8] The harvest of wheat was accompanied by the celebration of the Feast of Weeks (Exod 34:22), also called the Feast of the Wheat Harvest (Deut 16:10). This freewill offering commemorated deliverance from the bondage of Egypt.

The Feast of the Tabernacles

The final crops to be gathered were the fruit. Primarily this meant grapes, but figs and raisins were also harvested at that time.[9] The grape harvest in October was celebrated with the Feast of the Tabernacles (Deut 16:33). The tabernacles or booths were a reminder of Israel's time in the wilderness following the Exodus. This feast came at the end of the fruit harvest and thanked God for all of the bounty and blessings He had given His people.

Customs of Adoption, Marriage, and Restoration

The ancient Hebrew Law Codes make no mention of adoption.[10] Nevertheless, the concept of adoption plays a pivotal role in Ruth's world. Adoption in the modern sense of a court action was not what is meant by adoption in the Bible. In some cases, Israelites accepted the means of adoption expressed through other cultures such as the custom of barren women providing a slave as a secondary wife so that a child could be born into the family.[11] This was the case with Sarah, Leah, and Rachel. Also, any person who took in a child and gave moral instruction and physical shelter was also considered the adoptive parent. The reluctance of Ruth to leave Naomi is an indication of her status as an adopted daughter. Because the ceremony of adoption involved casting a garment over the one being adopted, Ruth's action at the threshing floor is seen by some theologians as an act of adoption (1 Kings 19:19; Ezek 16:8).[12]

Most commentaries, however, see Ruth's action at the threshing floor as an overture of marriage and a plea for a kinsman-redeemer. In Israel, the nearest relative occasionally took the place of the brother or kinsman who died so that the deceased man's property could be protected, and his widow could reap the financial benefit of her husband. This act was known as the kinsman-redeemer or *goʾel*. When the brother or kinsman agreed to buy back property that was sold by an impoverished man or his widow, that kinsman acted as a *goʾel* and redemption occurred. In Naomi's case, the *goʾel* was needed to redeem Elimelech's property and to restore Naomi (and Ruth) to good financial and community standing.

Ruth and Naomi's situation also called for a levirate marriage. In the case of a barren widow, marriage was necessary to preserve the legacy of the deceased husband's family. Naomi's family was in danger of losing their place of lineage in Israel. Elimelech had two sons, but both died childless. Through levirate law, a child could be born to another kinsman in the name of the deceased man. In Ruth's case, the child would bear the name of Mahlon, Ruth's husband, and therefore, restore the lineage of Naomi's family. Both redemption of the land and the securing of the lineage required the involvement of the nearest kinsman. Because Boaz was not the closest relative, he had to execute due diligence in seeking the nearest relative and securing the promise of redemption (Ruth 3:12; 4:3-8). Negotiation for the right of redemption took place at the city gate. This entrance was often the site of "the city market" and served as the central meeting place for those seeking justice or resolution of some legal issue.[13] When Boaz entered the city gate, he called an audience of the nearest kinsman and the elders who would serve as witnesses. Boaz was a shrewd negotiator. Before revealing the entire matter, Boaz told the nearest kinsman of the opportunity to purchase the land. The man may have been interested until Boaz presented the second half of the offer. This was an inclusion of the levirate law. In this arrangement, the property would belong to the family of the deceased man through that son. The nearest of kin had reason to be concerned. If he married Ruth and had a son that turned out to be his only son, then the kinsman's own inheritance (name) would be lost because the child would carry the name and represent the inheritance of the dead man rather than that of the new husband and actual father. The nearest kinsman refused to redeem the property saying, "I cannot redeem it for myself, lest I mar mine own inheritance" (Ruth 4:6).

At this point, another custom, *halizah,* came into play.[14] The removal of the shoe was an indication that the kinsman was declining to marry the widow and redeem the dead relative's property and name. The kinsman freed himself from the obligation to marry the widow by removing the shoe in the presence of witnesses, leaving the widow free to marry another kinsman in order to redeem the land.

GOD IN HER LIFE

Ruth began her life as a citizen in a polytheist nation. Despite her religious and cultural life in Moab, Ruth married into an Israelite family who worshiped Jehovah, the one true God of Israel.

Learning the Lord

In essence, the book of Ruth begins with Ruth learning who God is. Ruth's faith was birthed in Naomi's account of Hebrew history and God's deliverance. Her belief in the

God of Israel was sustained through her firsthand knowledge of how God kept Naomi through the deaths of her husband and her sons. In time, Ruth understood what God had done for Naomi's people and the importance of following Him no matter the circumstance. For Israel, hope in God preceded all else. Whether one experienced blessings or curses, God was to be praised. At Naomi's feet, Ruth learned to hope in the Lord, who had sustained Naomi regardless of the difficulties she faced. Thus, when Ruth went to Bethlehem-Judah, she was going as much with God as she was with her adoptive mother. Upon entering Judah, Ruth was not deterred by what appeared to be a bad situation. Instead, she was determined. God had delivered them from the land of Moab and had been with them through the arduous journey to Bethlehem. At this point, Ruth began to learn God for herself as she entered a new phase of understanding and trust.

The rituals of adoption that have been evident in the book of Ruth are highlighted in Ruth's acceptance of the God of Israel as Lord. "The stranger who enters into new religious relation with the Deity of his adopted land is said to come under the wings of the Deity whose protection he seeks."[15] In Moab, Ruth had been adopted by Naomi. In following her to Judah, Ruth adopted Jehovah as her God.

Following God

In Ruth 2:2, Ruth sought permission, much as a child might, to go into the fields to glean. In Ruth 2:10, Ruth referred to herself as "a stranger." She was still unaware of who Boaz was and very much aware that she was a new arrival to Judah. By chapter 3, Ruth understood that

God had provided abundantly for them through Boaz. In Ruth 3:3-4, Naomi gave Ruth specific instructions for approaching Boaz on the threshing floor. At the end of her instructions, Naomi tells Ruth to "go in, and uncover his feet, and lay thee down; and he will tell thee what thou shalt do." Ruth agreed. Verse six says that Ruth "did according to all that her mother in law bade her."

But Ruth was no longer a child. She had matured in her understanding of Hebrew customs and her new home. Ruth's arrival at the threshing floor was a turning point in her understanding of customs and relationships as well as her expression of faith. When Boaz noticed her at his feet, Ruth deviated from the instructions of her mother. Rather than responding in submissive and childlike obedience to Naomi's words, Ruth boldly declares "I am Ruth thine handmaid: spread therefore thy skirt over thine handmaid..."

In earlier references, Ruth is called "the Moabitess, (Naomi's) daughter in law" (Ruth 1:22) or "the Moabitish damsel that came back with Naomi" (Ruth 2:6). By stating simply, "I am Ruth," she declared herself to no longer be a stranger in a strange land. The customs and the people were no longer foreign to her. Ruth had an identity of her own. Her statement that she was "thine handmaid," proclaimed her relationship to the family of Boaz and Naomi. She was neither an outsider nor an in-law. Her greatest deviation from Naomi's instructions was in telling Boaz to "spread therefore thy skirt over thine handmaid; for thou art a near kinsman." Now aware of the custom and the intent, Ruth took charge of the situation. Through her statements, Ruth made it clear that the need for a kinsman-redeemer was now hers. She was no longer speaking on behalf of Naomi. She was seeking restoration of her dead husband's right to an inheritance through his father's land and the birth of a child in Mahlon's name.

Ruth's boldness took Boaz aback. He was elated that Ruth chose him, an older man, to be her provider and husband rather than seeking the favor of a young man of any wealth or status. Boaz was possibly also amazed at her boldness in declaring her desire that he undertake the obligation of the *go'el*. She identified Boaz and presented herself as the daughter seeking redemption for her mother as well as the woman seeking protection as a wife and family restoration through motherhood. Ruth was a follower of Jehovah, fully invested in Israel and her life in Bethlehem-Judah. She realized that the promise of restoration and redemption was fully hers because she was committed to the God of Israel.

Blessed and Highly Favored

Several blessings are spoken in the book of Ruth. Each shows God's grace in Ruth's life. In Ruth 1:8-9, Naomi blessed Ruth and Orpah saying, "the Lord deal kindly with you, as ye have dealt with the dead, and with me. The Lord grant you that ye may find rest, each of you in the house of her husband." In this farewell Naomi encouraged the two women to return to their mothers. This blessing confirmed that Ruth had been a good wife to Naomi's son. It foreshadowed the mercy and abundant grace Ruth would receive in Judah. While Ruth came to Judah to protect and provide for Naomi, the blessing by Naomi declared that all Ruth had done for her and her son would be returned by God as a blessing upon the younger woman. Naomi's blessing was also that "The Lord grant you that ye may find rest... in the house of (your) husband." Through the rites of the kinsman-redeemer and the levirate marriage, God fulfilled this blessing upon Ruth's life. Boaz was her husband, and his vow to raise a child unto Mahlon as well as to provide for Ruth and her mother was indeed a sign of rest.

The second blessing upon Ruth was spoken by Boaz. He prayed God's protection and provision for her in their first meeting (Ruth 2:11-12). He was the vehicle used by God to show kindness to her. He declared, "May the Lord, the God of Israel, under whose wings you have come to take refuge, reward you fully for what you have done" (NLT). In this blessing, Boaz referenced the adoptive power of God for those who seek Him. In leaving Moab, Ruth had begged Naomi not to make her return to her Moabite family.

...For whither thou goest, I will go; and where thou lodgest, I will lodge: thy people shall be my people, and thy God my God: Where thou diest, will I die, and there will I be buried: the Lord do so to me, and more also, if ought but death part thee and me. (Ruth 1:16-17)

Ruth declared her love for Naomi and her desire to continue as Naomi's adopted daughter. Through her declaration of adoptive love, Ruth proclaimed her trust in Jehovah and her denunciation of the gods of her native land and family. When Ruth left Moab, she did not know

God for herself; yet, she had confidence in Him based on Naomi's testimony and witness to His great power. Her statement that "thy people shall be my people," indicated that as the adopted daughter of Naomi, she would now be the adopted daughter of Jehovah. Ruth swore to live in the nation and among the people He delivered. Her oath was sealed when she stated, "the Lord do so to me, and more also, if ought but death part thee and me." The blessing that Boaz spoke over Ruth at their first meeting confirmed her covenant of love and commitment to Naomi and to God. At the threshing floor, Ruth again confirmed her commitment by proposing that Boaz be her husband, her provider, and the restorer of the inheritance. In marrying Boaz, Ruth's oath was fulfilled, and Boaz's blessing for God's adoptive grace was complete.

The people of Judah announced two blessings. The first occurred at the conclusion of the kinsman-redeemer ceremony.

> And all the people that were in the gate, and the elders, said, We are witnesses. The LORD make the woman that is come into thine house like Rachel and like Leah, which two did build the house of Israel: and do thou worthily in Ephratah, and be famous in Beth-lehem. (Ruth 4:11)

This was a confirmation of the grace shown to Ruth through the custom of the kinsman-redeemer. It was also a blessing that God would do more than restore the child as a memorial of inheritance to Mahlon. By referencing Rachel and Leah, the people were declaring that the child born through Ruth would be a blessing to the nation of Israel. This is a prophecy of the child who would carry prominence in the lineage of King David. No longer a stranger, this Moabite woman would carry the hope of Israel and the world through a lineage that would eventually reveal the Messiah (Matt 1:5).

The final blessing by the people came at the birth of the child born to Ruth through the levirate marriage as an inheritance to Mahlon. This blessing was spoken to Naomi but centered on Ruth.

> And the women said unto Naomi, Blessed be the Lord, which hath not left thee this day without a kinsman, that his name may be famous in Israel. And he shall be unto thee a restorer of thy life, and a nourisher of thine old age: for thy daughter in law, which loveth thee, which is better to thee than seven sons, hath born him. (Ruth 4:14-15)

The child, Obed, was the fulfillment of all Naomi desired. Through this blessing, the women declared that Ruth's adoptive action had been fulfilled. Her intent to be a true daughter to Naomi had been even greater than she could have imagined. Ruth was better than seven sons because it was the son born to her who would carry the name of the family and secure the inheritance of Ruth and Naomi. In this final blessing, and in the birth of Obed, we see Ruth reach full maturity as a follower of Jehovah.

WHAT HER LIFE SPEAKS

Ruth's life is a saga of faith and a rite of passage in God's blessing of those who were once strangers. Through Ruth, the promise of God for the redemption of the world is revealed, and all who hope in the Lord are given assurance of His faithfulness to those who seek protection under His wings.

Concept 1: The Lord Will Make A Way

In Ruth's life we see tragedy after tragedy; yet, through it all she lived in hope. Her husband died, but she found a mother whose God is a deliverer. The journey to Judah was arduous, but she made her way to a new land. She and her mother were poverty-stricken, but God gave her the mind to glean and the strength to gather the grain. She was a stranger in a strange land, but she was welcomed by those who met her. She was the least of all, but she was shown favor by all. She was born into a family and a home where the name of Jehovah was not known, but she learned God's name, depended upon His *hesed,* and was determined to follow His direction. Ruth's life echoes the words of an old Pentecostal refrain—"The Lord will make a way—somehow."

For women today, Ruth's life gives hope for a future greater than what is expected. In New Testament ideology, Ruth was a Gentile, a non-Jew who had no hope of redemption. She was a barren widow and an impoverished stranger. In case we think we cannot relate to Ruth's situation, Paul reminds the New Testament Christian as he writes, "…Ye were without Christ, … aliens from the commonwealth of Israel, and strangers from the covenants of promise, having no hope, and without God in the world" (Eph 2:12). Like Ruth, we were in need of God's protection, provision, and redemption. It is a true blessing that "Now in Christ Jesus ye who sometimes were far off are made nigh by the blood of Christ" (Eph 2:13).

Regardless of where life has taken us or brought us from, today's Christian can see in Ruth the possibilities that grow out of the impossible. Hope says that tomorrow will be better despite the fact that we cannot see beyond today. Ruth did not know she was going into Boaz's field, but the Lord made a way—somehow. Ruth had no idea that she would find a new husband. She was simply faithful to her commitment regarding the needs of Naomi. Despite their situation, the Lord made a way—somehow.

Not every idea and dream will come to pass in the life of the Christian. Not every unmarried woman will find the perfect husband. Not every woman will give birth to the child she desires. We may never get that ideal job or that glamorous home. Ruth's life does not present us with a checklist of possible outcomes. Her life gives us a pattern of faithful commitment to emulate. God did not make a way for Ruth because she was nice, generous, beautiful, or even diligent in her work. God made a way because Ruth was committed to following Him. She placed her focus and her hope on doing what she knew God was leading her to do. Her declaration of faith in Ruth 1:16-17 proclaimed her desire to follow God despite the fact she did not know what her future held. Whether she faced problems with lodging, relationships or death, she would do as God led because she was certain the Lord would make a way—somehow.

Concept 2: God Is Our Father
Ruth's visit to the threshing floor was her humbled request

for Boaz's recognition of her adoption into his clan. She had renounced her own father and mother and moved to an unknown place. In the wilderness of her life, she had sought the protection and covering of the only one who had shown her kindness, her adoptive mother, Naomi. Boaz's demonstration of love and care in providing protection and grain was like that of a father. In fact, Boaz's action foreshadows the nature of the coming Messiah and the essence of God. When Boaz visited the harvest fields in Ruth 2:4, he, like God, greeted the workers with new mercy that morning, new blessings for their day (Lam 3:22-23). Like God, Boaz did not sit so high that he did not look upon the lowly people who gleaned in the fields. He took note of the stranger, the foreigner, who had come to gather from his bounty. Not only did he notice Ruth, but upon hearing her name, he told her all about herself. Boaz knew the kindness she had shown Naomi and the distance she had traveled to be there. Like the omniscient God, he knew her past and he recognized her need. He saw her future in a new land.

Through Boaz, we see how God is a gracious Father to all. He sees our need. When we feel lost, lonely, confused, hurting, hungry, and disquieted in our spirits, God sees us. His provision does not happen just as we arrive at a point to acknowledge him. In Jeremiah 1:5, we learn that God knew us and called us even before we were born. The sum of *His* wealth cannot be told; His riches are beyond our understanding. Just as Boaz covered Ruth, God covers us and adopts us into His family.

Concept 3: God Is Our Provider
We see a moving example of God's provision in Boaz's ac-

tions toward Ruth. In Ruth 2:14, Boaz provided the bread Ruth needed for daily sustenance. In verses 16 and 17, he instructed the keeper of the harvest fields to give her "handfuls on purpose" so that her cup literally ran over with an entire "ephah of barley." By instructing her to follow those who gleaned in his fields each day and not to go to another field, he vowed to provide for her and Naomi every day and to protect her journey. When Ruth met Boaz on the threshing floor, he gave her "six measures" more of barley so that she could share it with Naomi.

As Christians, we read this encounter and are reminded of Jesus, who fed the 5,000. His simple loaves of barley provided more than enough for the crowd. In the Passover meal, barley represents the deliverance provided to Israel by a righteous God. The barley Boaz so freely gave Ruth showed his desire to deliver her from the poverty that plagued her life. His concern was not only for her physical hunger but her total life. Likewise, God cares about our physical, mental, emotional, and even social needs. He provides a place of shelter and a table from which we may freely feast. As He did with Ruth, God sees that we are in relationship with those who can show us the way to follow Him and to stay in His field forever.

Boaz provided food for Ruth and Naomi, but in doing so he also gave them hope. When Ruth met Boaz he immediately provided her with enough to take care of herself and Naomi, but he had a desire to do even more. It was upon the threshing floor that he declared his willingness to redeem Ruth and all that pertained to her and Naomi. The hope provided to them through Boaz's actions reminds us of the hope we have through Jesus

Christ. For most Christians, the determination to follow Christ comes on the heels of pain that signals a need for His love. Whether our tears come from disappointment in friends or disagreements with family, we become acutely aware that the situation is beyond our ability to rectify. When our tears come from facing difficult economic struggles, attempting to cope with a devastating diagnosis or even experiences with the death of a loved one, they make us call on Jesus Christ as our Savior. In those times of challenge, we learn to trust God fully for deliverance and provision. In those hard times, as in the good times, we seek God's grace and mercy as demonstrations of His continued faithfulness and the fulfillment of His promise of deliverance. Our faith in God and His faithfulness toward us gives us hope for tomorrow and makes today brighter.

Concept 4: Jesus Christ Is Our Redeemer
Ruth's quest for God was demonstrated in her desire to follow God even to the end of the earth as she knew it. She repented of her former life and left behind the false gods of her nation and her family. Like Abraham, Ruth went to a place that God showed her. This was a place she had not known, a place where the promises of God would come to pass. Ruth's journey to Judah was more than a physical transition. It was an emotional and spiritual shedding of her past, a coming of age in faith and commitment to God. The witness of her mother-in-law through words and deeds was enough to show Ruth that God was faithful to those who sought Him and who came under His wing.

In the Old Testament, God was seen as *goʾel,* the one closest in kinship who could secure their immediate and future rights. Boaz's decision to serve as nearest kin made the legal case for Ruth's property and her hand in marriage. The faith Naomi and Ruth had in Boaz's ability and desire to deliver them from their condition of poverty was based on their faith that God would hear their prayers. Through Boaz, the book of Ruth provides a stunning and moving projection of Jesus Christ as our Kinsman-Redeemer, the One who fulfills the Old Testament foreshadowing of God's *hesed*. In Christ, the promise of the *go'el* is complete. Matthew 6:33 admonishes us to "Seek the Kingdom of God above all else, and live righteously, and he will give you everything you need" (NLT). The born-again believer recognizes that the right of redemption was solidified on Calvary through Jesus Christ. Through Jesus Christ, our impoverished lives of sin have been redeemed. Our status as strangers and outcasts from the protection, grace, and love of God has been removed. All that pertains to us has been secured through Him. Christ calls us to seek Him first and to recognize our citizenship in His Kingdom. Everything else will follow because Jesus Christ has already been declared our Kinsman-Redeemer.

Hearing Ruth

WHAT YOUR LIFE SPEAKS

Speak Your Truth

1. If there is a label to be given, Ruth could wear it. She was a stranger, an orphan, a widow, and a poor person. On the other hand, she was generous, obedient, humble, and faithful. Many times society, families, and others place labels on us that define us to others—and sometimes to ourselves. What labels have been put on you and by whom?

2. If you identified a label (or labels), how have those descriptions helped or hurt you? Do you agree with them? If not, what would be your first step in changing them?

Focus Your Faith

1. Matthew 6:33 says, "Seek ye first the kingdom of God, and his righteousness; and all these things shall be added unto you." This Scripture is a call to faith. Have you sought God's kingdom first? How?

2. If you are struggling to embrace Matthew 6:33, why? What hinders you from fully accepting this invitation? Where can you turn for help?

USING YOUR VOICE

Ponder

1. God had a future for Ruth that was beyond her expectations. Jeremiah 29:11 says, "For I know the thoughts

that I think toward you, saith the LORD, thoughts of peace, and not of evil, to give you an expected end." What plans do you believe God has for you?

2. How are you yielding to God's will rather than operating from your own desires?

Pray

1. Jesus Christ is our Kinsman-Redeemer. Pray a prayer of thanksgiving for the redemption you have received through Christ's sacrifice.

2. If you have not been redeemed by Jesus Christ and do not know Him as your Savior, the opportunity is available at this moment. Seek the indwelling of the Holy Spirit now and ask God to cover you with His protective grace and mercy.

Practice

1. If you have loved ones or friends who do not know Christ as Savior, share this discussion with them. Help them recognize Jesus as Kinsman-Redeemer, who paid the price for their salvation.

2. Thousands of children in each state in the U.S. are in foster care. Some are in good homes; others live in abusive situations or on the street. Contact a local agency and ask what you can do to help increase awareness of this problem or address a need.

Speak, Lord

TOO OFTEN Bible "lessons" are heavy on David and Paul but scarce on Dinah and Anna. There are nearly 200 women mentioned in the Bible. We are familiar with only a few. Figures such as Eve, Deborah, Hannah, and at least two women named Mary come to mind easily. There are other women in the Bible whose names are either not mentioned or too obscure to remember. At points, prototypes of women suffice such as the virtuous woman of Proverbs 31. If we begin with the premise that the Bible is the inspired Word of God, then even the not-very-virtuous women like Jezebel should not be overlooked. Women are present in the Bible, but a failure to examine their cultural and social histories makes them either predictable or invisible. God desires us to notice the women. To do that, we must read the Bible while posing a key question: "Women, where are you?"

Let Her Life Speak is a call for modern readers to hear the voices of women in the Bible. They speak with inspired hope. However, our failure to dig deeply into these women's lives and social locations has distorted or dismissed their messages. Each of the women highlighted in this volume provides a revelation about God. Each provides a vision that will enhance our journeys as we seek to live as faithful witnesses of Jesus Christ. But hearing their messages requires us to find the women behind the text. These women and others speak to us, but we must be willing to ask, "Women, where are you?" We must seek them out. Hearing their voices requires that we identify each as someone from whom we can glean God's will and His warnings for our lives and our times.

Hearing a Prophetic Word from Old Testament Women
Old Testament prophets included women and men. *Let Her Life Speak* does not attempt to assign any prophetic office to the women in this volume. That would be an error; yet, the messages of these Bible women provide a prophetic word for today's Christians. Old Testament prophets employed "a variety of speech forms including... oracles."[1] An oracle is a communication that explains a God-centered principle, warning, or hope. It is a method of explaining God's will and of sharing divine wisdom. Oracles are spoken and meant to be heard. The purpose of this volume is to clarify the oracles of these women. The messages highlighted in each discussion provide prophetic understandings of God in the lives of people. The

God-centered principles, warnings, and hope raised here shed light on God's will and provide wisdom for a new generation.

Author and theologian Tikva Frymer-Kensky speaks of specific biblical women as prophets. Rahab, she says, is among those women "pressed into service as 'onetime' prophets to both mark and participate in the making of Israel's history. Without Rahab, the spies would not have returned her words of certainty and the Israelites might not have been so willing to cross the Jordan."[2] The women highlighted in *Let Your Life Speak* are not categorized as oracles or prophets, but their messages present prophetic utterances. As Frymer-Kensky writes, "Together these women outline the history of Israel, punctuating it with reminders that this story was shaped and foretold by God." These women are heard at "turning points" in the life of Israel. Their oracles are presented "by their existence…, (and) their messages (show) the direction in which Israel will move."[3] Each of the women in *Let Her Life Speak* gives us a message shaped by God for their time and ours.

As author Carolyn Sharp states, "God has acted in history! This is something the prophets proclaim over and over again. God spoke to real people in ancient Israel and transformed the lives of real communities…. But we need to listen."[4] Sharp describes the prophet as a "truth-teller… a compelling figure in the spiritual imagination of ancient Israel, the Christian church, and secular culture."[5] As we examine the lives of the women in this book, Sharp's concepts trigger our spiritual imaginations through three "diverse and distinctive messages of biblical prophets."[6] Each of the women in this volume can be viewed from at least one of these perspectives.

1. The prophets are mediators of God's holiness in the world. "Holiness is what God is."[7] "The prophet's task is to mediate God's holiness to a world that cannot fully understand it and doesn't know how to accommodate it..."[8] The prophetic word calls us to recognize God's holiness. Doing so compels us to examine our relationship to an irreverent world and then position ourselves to serve this holy God. This is the prophetic message of Naomi's life. Despite the trials she faced, Naomi always saw God as holy and without blame. Through Naomi's faith, we recognize God's holiness and His *hesed,* which is His loving kindness, mercy, commitment, and peace in our lives. Through Naomi's struggle, we learn to appreciate the necessity of *hesed* in our relationships with others and to see *hesed* as an outpouring of God's holiness. Naomi's life invites us to trust God.

It is through Ruth that we recognize the willingness of a holy God to save and restore sinful humanity. Like Ruth, who was a stranger in Judah, we all come to God as individuals who "were without Christ, being aliens from the commonwealth of Israel, and strangers from the covenants of promise, having no hope, and without God in the world" (Eph 2:12). As we hear of God's holiness through Ruth's life, we are drawn "as newborn babes, (who) desire the sincere milk of the word, that (we) may grow thereby" (1 Peter 2:2). Ruth's life encourages us to cultivate a relationship with God and reassures us that this holy God can and will deliver.

2. *The prophets are idealists.* As Sharp explains, prophets "will not let us rest content with inadequate understandings of God. They urge us to deeper reflection on obedience, love, and justice. They exhort us to practice what they preach."[9] Leah delivers this prophetic message when she grapples with family relationships that deny her personhood. Through Leah, we see a progressive understanding of who God is and what He expects. Just as Jacob wrestled with the angel until he received his blessing, Leah wrestles with her understanding of God. In Leah's quest, we come to expect the ideal. Through her, we realize that even if we fail to understand God's actions, we can trust Him for the revelation of His ideal self. Leah's prophetic utterances through the names of her children lead us to embrace the life that a loving God has ordained for us—a life that is "exceeding abundantly above all that we ask or think, according to the power that worketh in us" (Eph 3:20).

Through Esther's life, we search for the ideal in justice and obedience. Despite the circumstances that called her to the throne of Persia, Esther's journey teaches us that we must persevere for the truth of what God wants from our lives. As we examine Esther's life, we recognize the need to overcome our fear and hesitation in order to live in obedience to God's will. Esther's call for spiritual discipline and social justice reminds us that God's purpose is greater than our comfort, and His will is far beyond our comprehension. Her life encourages us to "come boldly unto the throne of grace, that we may obtain mercy, and find grace to help in time of need" (Heb 4:16).

3. The prophets are our companions. "The prophets know that God loves us. So the prophets can stand with us in solidarity, encouraging us to rejoice in God's mercy and warning us when we stray from God's way."[10] Bathsheba's pain and loss remind us that life is difficult and sometimes unbearable. Yet, her commitment to the promise of her son's future prompts us to recall that God will never leave us nor forsake us (Heb 13:5). In our deepest pain and our darkest sorrows, Bathsheba reminds us that we must be faithful to the God, who knows our history and our future. Similarly, in the lives of Vashti and Rahab, non-Israelite women, we see that God has a plan that is based solely on His mercy. Their lives point the way to victory even in the face of doubt and trial. The lives of Bathsheba, Vashti, and Rahab tell us that our lives matter and that with God on our side we have influence from generation to generation.

Searching for Prophetic Revelation through New Testament Women

Although *Let Her Life Speak* has deliberately presented

the lives of seven Old Testament women, we cannot forget that New Testament women also reveal avenues of faith through God's presence in their lives. It might be argued that New Testament women are more visible and available to readers than their Old Testament counterparts. However, without a deliberate attempt to find these women, their prophetic voices may be lost to us as well. The question, "Women, where are you?" is still relevant in our search for prophetic voices through New Testament study.

New Testament prophecy has two categories. The first type of prophetic word is heard through the voices of the apostles. The second "type of prophetic activity" does not claim to be "the very word of God, but...was for 'strengthening, encouragement and comfort' of believers (1 Cor 14:3)."[11] An example from Paul's Second Missionary Journey demonstrates how easily we can overlook New Testament women and their prophetic encounters with struggle and faith.

Paul's second trip was designed to revisit the churches established during his First Missionary Journey. He reasoned: "Let us go again and visit our brethren in every city where we have preached the word of the Lord, and see how they do" (Acts 15:36). That second trip, however, differed from what Paul expected. Silas rather than Barnabas accompanied Paul in the visit "through Syria and Cilicia, confirming the churches" (Acts 15:41). Even the decision of where to go was not Paul's. The greatest deviation in the journey took place when "a vision appeared to Paul in the night... saying, Come over into Macedonia, and help us" (Acts 16:9).

Paul's method of ministry always began in the synagogue. It was customary for the leader of the synagogue to select the Scripture reading for the day and offer strangers in attendance the opportunity to share in the discussion. This was a natural segue into the gospel message. By tradition, it took only ten married men to establish a synagogue.[12] Because Paul's methodology had proven successful, he planned to continue the pattern of beginning his evangelistic message by preaching in the synagogue when he journeyed to Philippi in Macedonia. But after remaining in Philippi for several days, Paul found no synagogue. Custom dictated that when there were too few Jewish men to have a synagogue, Jews went to the river for prayer and ritual washing.[13] At that point, Paul and those who traveled with him went to the nearby river in search of a few good men with whom to start his ministry of the Word. Once there, however, Paul realized there were no men at the river. Instead, he found a group of Gentile women. While Paul was not looking for women, the Holy Spirit was presenting the answer to the critical question, "Women, where are you?"

Paul's experience at Philippi gives us a glimpse into the importance of women in the Bible and the critical role God has for women in the Gospel journey today. In recording the events at the river, the Holy Spirit led Dr. Luke to single out one woman—Lydia, who is popularly known as "a seller of purple" (Acts 16:14). The material she sold was valuable and made her a wealthy woman with servants and a large house. But Lydia's presence at the river's edge is not about prosperity. It is about faith and spiritual gifting. While Paul had not been looking for the women, God wanted the women to hear the call to salvation and to help move the message of Jesus Christ into a new culture and region as the door in Macedonia was opened.

Like Paul, the search for New Testament women forces us to pause at the river to hear Lydia's prophetic word. After Lydia and her household responded to the gospel preached by Paul, she immediately offered the gift of hospitality that God had already nurtured in her. With prophetic understanding, Lydia pleaded with Paul to share her home, her food, and her resources (Acts 16:15). At their meeting, Lydia had no idea that Paul and Silas would be beaten and imprisoned (Acts 16:22-23). She had no way of knowing that the newly birthed church at Philippi would need a place to meet (Acts 16:40). But by answering the call of God, she was in a position to offer all she had to the work of the ministry. Lydia's prophetic utterance causes us reflect on the gifts and abilities the Holy Spirit has already bestowed and nurtured in our lives. Lydia's presence encourages us to heed God's call to salvation, to offer ourselves in service to God, and to recognize the gifts of grace He has already given us.

Like most Bible readers, Paul was not looking for women. However, Paul was open to going where the Spirit led him. Had he been resistant or determined to continue his plan, he would have missed an opportunity to spread the gospel and engage women in the effort. When our study of the Bible asks, "Women, where are you?" we must investigate the lives of the women we find in God's Word. Without posing that question, we will continue to pass by Lydia and the women at the river to see what Paul would do next.

Valuing Women Today

When we ask, "Women, where are you?" we are not saying that women are hiding or that God is clueless about their presence in the Bible or the world. It is instead an appeal to individuals, as well as the church, to re-examine the lives of women in the Bible for a fresh understanding of the importance of women to the message of God. We must ask, "Women, where are you?" because knowing the women in the Bible and hearing their prophetic voices causes us to be mindful of the ministry of God's grace to women. It requires us to re-evaluate our understanding, thinking, and attitudes about the women of the Bible and the importance of women in the church. There are several aspects of valuing women we must address.

First, God is calling all Christians to reconsider the place we have assigned to women in the body of Christ. God called women just as he called men; He sees no difference (Galatians 3:28). God has equipped both men and women for His glory. Spiritual gifts are given by God for the edification of the church. Yet, despite God's plan to engage both genders, some denominations forbid women to enter the clergy. In other cases, women are only permitted to teach children, not adults and definitely not men. Even when a call to ministry is acknowledged, ordination credentials may be denied. When congregations and individuals restrict these gifts or limit involvement based on gender, they hinder the work of the gospel and fail to meaningfully connect the biblical models with the power of God in human lives.

Second, the prophetic utterances of Bible people give credibility to the lives of Christians without regard to gender. Through the female—and male—voices in the Bible, we understand God's vision for men and women to be in relationship with His divine grace. We have learned to hear the voices of biblical men, and we have committed their situations and circumstances to memory. When we add the question of "Women, where are you?" we realize that the productive lives of women in the church cannot be fully realized until we heed the prophetic voices of women in the Bible and address issues that stymy the voices of our sisters today.

Third, women themselves have a powerful role to play in engaging women in the body of Christ. We can no longer ignore the harm that comes to women and young girls when the general ethos accepts excuses for why women fail to support their sisters. If women embrace the lessons of sisterhood, leadership, and community through the lens of Bible women, they are likely to rethink their own perspectives. One problem is the division of people into arbitrary categories of isolation. Christians today talk about "destinies" and "next-level thinking" in terms of material gain, wealth, or positional power. *Let Her Life Speak* has identified Bible women of varying economic and social backgrounds who challenge our ideas about success and purpose. Entrepreneurs like Rahab and Lydia shatter our prototypes of who can succeed to assure us that our success is anchored in our embrace of God's will for our lives. Leah, Naomi, and Ruth may appear to be women whose struggles overshadow their possibilities, but their lives tell us that trusting God and growing in our knowledge of Him are the paths to the goals that are most important in our lives. While Bathsheba, Esther, and Vashti could undoubtedly win the contest for "Palace Beauties," our journey into their lives reveals the importance of using our voices to declare God's truth and secure justice for ourselves and others.

When we examine the lives of Bible women and appropriate their prophetic words for today, our perspective changes. Studying the lives of these women helps us realize the depth of their commitment and the breadth of their involvement in the work of the Lord. When we examine the lives of Bible women and listen to their voices through the text, we learn the worth and vibrancy of our roles in the body of Christ and are liberated to resist the stereotypes attributed to Christian women today.

A public service announcement asked people to demonstrate what it means to "run like a girl." For many adults, there was a marked difference between how girls run and how boys run. Adult men and women depicted running by boys as powerful and deliberate in movement. Girls, however, were described as moving in impotent and flailing ways that showed little purpose and even less impact. When young girls were asked what it meant to "run like a girl," they described running as "going as fast as you can." They saw no gender difference.

This same question could be asked in the church: What does it mean to worship and serve God as a woman? Answer: There should be no gender difference in our worship or our service. *Let Her Life Speak* has attempted to address this idea by exploring how women's lives speak through the pages of the Bible. Our renewed understanding of the importance of Bible women leaves us with three calls to action:

- **Deeper Study** – The call for a deeper study of God's Word includes learning from both genders. When we expand our quest to incorporate the lives of biblical women and men in our study of God's Word, we better see God's hand and more easily surrender to His will.

- **Greater Access** – Having greater access to female role models in biblical contexts allows Christian women to respond more faithfully to spiritual realities. Women have always experienced the joys and pains of life in everything from childbirth to death, from cherished relationships to tragic separations. While the context of modern lives is totally different from the world of Bible women, the emotional and spiritual complexities are similar and provide valuable keys to faithful living.

- **Richer Service** – It is necessary for women to serve the church fully as an expression of their journeys of faith. In a world where chaos often seems to reign, women cannot hide their heads or allow their lives and gifts to be artificially restricted. God calls women as well as men to "do justly, and to love mercy, and to walk humbly with thy God" (Micah 6:8). When the question is asked, "Women, where are you?" today's Christian women, like the women of the Bible, must be present and ready to say, "Here I am, Lord. Send me" (Isaiah 6:8).

Hearing the Lord

WHAT YOUR LIFE SPEAKS

Speak Your Truth

1. It is important to have "truth-tellers" in our lives who can give honest encouragement, strength, and warning on a personal level. Who do you trust to fulfill this role in your life?

2. How has *Let Her Life Speak* encouraged and supported your effort to dig into God's Word more deeply?

Focus Your Faith

1. Select at least one Bible woman from this book and explain how her actions and/or interactions with God are encouraging to your life.

2. It is important to discern God's call on your life. What dreams, visions, and ideas has God placed in your heart that will help you serve the Kingdom?

USING YOUR VOICE

Ponder

1. What have you learned about the importance of seeking women's voices in the Word of God?

2. This discussion has positioned the women in *Let Her Life Speak* as prophetic voices. Do you agree or disagree? Why?

Pray

1. Pray for women who are limited or feel limited in ex-

ercising God's call on their lives. Pray that these women will find the freedom to operate in their call to service and the courage of spiritual wholeness.

2. God calls us to present our bodies as living sacrifices, holy, acceptable unto God, which is our reasonable service (Romans 12:1). How are you doing this? Ask God to strengthen you in this area. Pray, also, for someone you know is struggling with presenting her body, gifts, talents, and will to God.

Practice

1. Identify a woman you can mentor or that you wish to have as a mentor. Cultivate the relationship by explaining the positive qualities and potential she represents to you.
2. Identify a woman in the Bible who was not discussed in this book. Conduct your own study of her life. Use the format of this book as a guide. Compile a list of the truths you gain from her voice.

End Notes

Preface — Listening to Bible Voices with Heart and Mind
1. The Barna Group, "Sunday School is Changing in Under-the-Radar But Significant Ways," http://www.barna.org/barna-update/article/5-barna-update/175-sunday-school-is-changing-in-under-the-radar-but-significant-ways?q=educational+sunday+school (accessed 5/17/2012).

Discussion 1 — Bathsheba
1. Hershel Shanks, ed., Ancient Israel, (Washington, DC: Prentice Hall and Biblical Archaeology Society, 1999), 164.
2. Steven L. McKenzie, "2 Samuel," in The New Oxford Annotated Bible, (New York: Oxford University Press, 2010), 446.
3. Shanks, 106.
4. Rebecca Harris, "Does God Engage in Rape? Rape as a Military Motif in the Prophets," in Pax Pneuma: The Journal of Pentecostal and Charismatics of Peace and Justice, 5 (2009): 8.
5. Jon D. Levenson, "Genesis," in The Jewish Study Bible, (2004): 69.
6. Shimon Bar-Efrat, "2 Samuel," in The Jewish Study Bible, (2004): 640.
7. Harris, 9.
8. "Hittite" in The Jewish Encyclopedia Online, http://jewishencyclopedia.com/articles/7774-hittites (accessed November 12, 2014).
9. Harris, 13.

Discussion 2 — Leah
1. Victor Matthews, Manners and Customs in the Bible, (Peabody, MA: Hendrickson Publishers, 1988), 133.
2. Fred H. Wright, Manners and Customs of Bible Lands, (Chicago: Moody Press, 1953), 124-134.
3. "Laban," in Jewish Encyclopedia Online, http://jewishencyclopedia.com/articles/9568-laban (accessed November 5, 2014).
4. Hershel Shanks, ed., Ancient Israel, (Washington, DC: Prentice Hall and Biblical Archaeology Society, 1999), 165.
5. Gordon-Conwell Theological Seminary, "Custom and Law in Ancient Mesopotamia," in NIV Archaeological Study Bible, (Grand

Rapids, MI: Zondervan, 2005) 36.

6. Walter A. Ewell, ed., "Concubines," in Baker Theological Dictionary of the Bible, (Grand Rapids, MI: Baker Book House, 1996) 110.

7. W. E. Shewell-Cooper, "Mandrakes," in GLO Premium Electronic Bible, (Orlando, FL: Immersion Digital, Inc., 2010).

8. Robert Alter, "Genesis," note 18 in The Five Books of Moses, (New York: W. W. Norton, 2004) 161.

9. Elvina M. Hall, "Jesus Paid I All," in The New National Baptist Hymnal, (Nashville, TN: National Baptist Publishing Board, 1977/1998), 89.

Discussion 3 — Esther

1. Lillian Klein is among the scholars who believe that "Ahaseurus's name may have been a title: "chief of rulers." Lillian R, Klein, From Deborah to Esther, (Minneapolis, MN: Augsburg Fortress, 2003), 98.

2. Klein, 103.

3. Klein, 102-103.

4. Adele Berlin, "Esther: Introduction," in Jewish Study Bible, (Oxford: University Press, 2004), 1625.

5. Berlin, 1623.

6. "The Canonicity of Esther," in NIV Archaeological Study Bible, (Grand Rapids, MI: Zondervan, 2005), 730.

7. Jeanne Porter, Leading Ladies, (Minneapolis, MN: Augsburg Books, 2005) 72.

8. "Counselors, Concubines: Life in an Ancient Royal Palace in NIV Archaeological Study Bible, 719.

9. "Daniel," note 1:7, in NIV Archaeological Study Bible, 1384.

10. Klein, 101.

11. "Haman," in Jewish Encyclopedia Online, http://jewishencyclopedia.com/articles/7124-haman-the-agagite (accessed 1/13/2015).

12. Klein, 104.

13. Klein, 107.

Discussion 4 — Vashti

1. "Susa," in NIV Archaeology Study Bible, (Grand Rapids: Zondervan, 2005) 729.

2. "The King's Gate," in NIV Archaeology Study Bible, 722.

3. "Counselors and Concubines: Life in an Ancient Royal Palace," in NIV Archaeology Study Bible, 719.

4. Rabbi David E. Eidensohn, Secret of the Scale, https://video.search.yahoo.com/video/play;_ylt=A2KLqIXW7N1UUw0ASx-L7w8QF;_ylu=X3oDMTByYXI3cnIwBHNlYwNzcgRzbGsDdm-

lkBHZ0aWQDBGdwb3MDNA--?p=queen+vashti&vid=5d-254fb79a02cceb191a7f9948f67b02&l=8%3A11&turl=http%3A%2F%2Fts4.mm.bing.net%2Fth%3Fid%3DVN.60799940 1996517923%26pid%3D15.1&rurl=https%3A%2F%2Fwww.youtube.com%2Fwatch%3Fv%3DEeYTFSIvtp4&tit=Persian+Queen+Vashti+is+Killed+2500+years+ago+-+The+first+feminism%3F&c=3&sigr=11bp915fp&sigt=1234jd46i&sigi=11rdfstbo&age=1236790528&fr2=p%3As%2Cv%3Av&fr=yfp-t-319&tt=b (accessed 1/30/2015)
5. http://www.merriam-webster.com/dictionary/authentic

Discussion 5 — Rahab
1. Othello (excerpt from Act 2, Scene 3, page 12) in Spark Notes at http://nfs.sparknotes.com/othello/page_110.html (accessed 6/9/2015)
2. Translations researched at biblegateway.com (accessed 3/8/2015).
3. "Rahab" in Jewish Encyclopedia Online, http://jewishencyclopedia.com/articles/12535-rahab (Accessed 3/8/2015).
4. W. E. Shewell-Cooper, "Flax," in Glo Bible Electronic Premium Edition, (Orlando, FL: Immersion Digital, Inc., 2010).
5. "The Walls of Jericho," in NIV Archaeological Study Bible (Grand Rapids, MI: Zondervan, 2005) 312.
6. Ibid, 312.
7. Tikva Frymer-Kensky, "Woman as Voice" in Reading the Women of the Bible (ebook), (New York: Schocken Books, 2002) 327.

Discussion 6 — Naomi
1. "Moab," in NIV Archaeological Study Bible, (Grand Rapids, MI: Zondervan, 2005) 292.
2. J. Lilley, "Ruth," in Glo Bible Electronic Premium Edition, (Orlando, FL: Immersion Digital, Inc., 2010) Note 4:3.
3. Leila Leah Bronner, "Stories of Biblical Mothers: Maternal Power in the Hebrew Bible" http://www.bibleandjewishstudies.net/articles/biblicalmothers.htm (accessed January 20, 2015)
4. Ian Duguid, "Loyal-Love," http://www.ligonier.org/learn/articles/loyal-love-hesed/ (accessed February 1, 2015).

Discussion 7 — Ruth
1. "Weddings in Ancient Israel," in NIVArchaeological Study Bible, (Grand Rapids, MI: Zondervan, 2005) 1039.
2. H. M. Wolf, "Harvest," in Glo Bible Electronic Premium Edition, (Orlando, FL: Immersion Digital, Inc., 2010).

3. E. Russell, "Gleaning, Glean," in Glo Bible.

4. G. B. Funderburk, "Threshing Floor," in Glo Bible; "Harvest," in Jewish Encyclopedia, http://jewishencyclopedia.com/articles/7297-harvest; "The Threshing Floor" in Archaeological Study Bible, 608.

5. "Food and Agriculture," in NIV Archaeological Study Bible, 396; J. H. Paterson, "Seasons," in Glo Bible.

6. "Barley" in Jewish Encyclopedia, http://jewishencyclopedia.com/articles/2531-barley (accessed January 12, 2015); S. Barabas, "Barley Harvest," in Glo Bible.

7. "Harvest" in Jewish Encyclopedia, http://jewishencyclopedia.com/articles/7297-harvest (accessed January 10, 2015).

8. "Wheat" in Jewish Encyclopedia, http://jewishencyclopedia.com/articles/14886-wheat (accessed January 12, 2015); H. M. Wolf, "Harvest," in Glo Bible.

9. H. M. Wolf, "Harvest," in Glo Bible.

10. A. H. Leitch, "Adoption," in Glo Bible.

11. "Nuzi," in Archaeological Study Bible, 52.

12. "Adoption," in Jewish Encyclopedia, http://jewishencyclopedia.com/articles/852-adoption (accessed February 5, 2015).

13. S. Barabas, "Gate," in Glo Bible; "The City Gate" in Archaeological Study Bible, 392.

14. "Halizah," in Jewish Encyclopedia, http://jewishencyclopedia.com/articles/7105-halizah (accessed January 10, 2015).

15. "Adoption," in Jewish Encyclopedia, http://jewishencyclopedia.com/articles/852-adoption (accessed February 5, 2015).

Discussion 8 — Speak, Lord

1. Karl Moller, "Prophecy and Prophets in the Old Testament," in Dictionary of Theological Interpretation, (Grand Rapids, MI: Baker Academic, 2005) 626-627.

2. Tikva Fryme-Kensky, "Woman as Voice" in Reading the Women of the Bible (e-book), (Grand Rapids, MI: Schocken Books, 2002) 327.

3. Fryme-Kensky, 327

4. Carolyn Sharp, "What Is a Prophet," in Old Testament Prophets for Today, (Louisville, KY: Westminster John Knox Press, 2009) 17-18.

5. Sharp, 2-3.

6. Sharp, 15.

7. M. William Ury. "Holiness" in Baker Theological Dictionary of the Bible, (Grand Rapids, MI: Baker Books, 1996) 341.

8. Sharp, 15.

9. Sharp, 16.

10. Sharp, 17.

11. Walter Kaiser, "Prophet, Prophetess, Prophecy," in Baker Theological Dictionary, 646.

12. W. White, Jr., "Synagogue," in Glo Bible Electronic Premium Edition (Orlando, FL: Immersion Digital, Inc., 2010).

13. "Acts" Note 16:13 in NIV Archaeological Study Bible (Grand Rapids, MI: Zondervan, 2005) 16:13 note.

References

Alter, Robert. *The Five Books of Moses: Genesis*.
New York: W. W. Norton, 2004

The Barna Group, "Sunday School is Changing in Under-the-Radar But Significant Ways" http://www.barna.org/barna-update/article/5-barna-up-date/175-sunday-school-is-changing-in-under-the-ra-dar-but-significant-ways?q=educational+sunday+school (accessed 5/17/2012).

Berlin, Adele. *Esther: Introduction. In Jewish Study Bible*.
Oxford: University Press, 2004.

Bronner, Leila Leah. *Stories of Biblical Mothers: Maternal Power in the Hebrew Bible*. Available: http://www. bibleandjewishstudies.net/articles/bibli-calmothers.htm.

The Canonicity of Esther. In NIV Archaeological
Study Bible. Grand Rapids, MI: Zondervan, 2005.

Duguid, Ian. Loyal-Love. Available: http://www.ligonier.org/learn/articles/loyal-love-hesed.

Eidensohn, Rabbi David E. *Secret of the Scale*. Available:
https://video.search.yahoo.com/video/play;_

ylt=A2KLqIXW7N1UUw0ASxL7w8QF;_ylu=X3oDMT-
ByYXI3cnIwBHNlYwNzcgRzbGsDdmlkBHZ0aWQDB-
Gdwb3MDNA--?p=queen+vashti&vid=5d254fb79a02c-
ceb191a7f9948f67b02&l=8%3A11&turl=http%3A%2F
%2Fts4.mm.bing.net%2Fth%3Fid%3DVN.607999401
996517923%26pid%3D15.1&rurl=https%3A%2F%2F-
www.youtube.com%2Fwatch%3Fv%3DEeYTFSIvt-
p4&tit=Persian+Queen+Vashti+is+Killed+2500+-
years+ago+-+The+first+feminism%3F&c=3&sig-
r=11bp915fp&sigt=1234jd46i&sigi=11rdfst-
bo&age=1236790528&fr2=p%3As%2Cv%3Av&fr=y-
fp-t-319&tt=b

Ewell, Walter A. *Concubines. In Baker Theological Dictionary of the Bible.* Grand Rapids, MI: Baker Book House, 1996.

Frymer-Kensky, Tikva. *Woman as Voice. In Reading the Women of the Bible (ebook),* New York: Schocken Books, 2002.

Glo Bible Electronic Premium Edition. Orlando, FL: Immersion Digital, Inc., 2010.

Gordon-Conwell Theological Seminary. *Custom and Law in Ancient Mesopotamia. In NIV Archaeological Study Bible.* Grand Rapids, MI: Zondervan, 2005.

Harris, Rebecca. *Does God Engage in Rape? Rape as a Military Motif in the Prophets.* In Pax Pneuma: The

Journal of Pentecostal and Charismatics of Peace and Justice, Vol. 5, 2009

Jewish Encyclopedia Online. Available: http://jewishencyclopedia.com/articles/7124-haman-the-agagite

The Jewish Publication Society. *Jewish Study Bible.* New York: Oxford University Press, 2004.

Kaiser, Walter. *Prophet, Prophetess, Prophecy.* In Baker Theological Dictionary. Grand Rapids, MI: Baker Books, 1996.

Klein, Lillian. *From Deborah to Esther.* Minneapolis, MN: Augsburg Fortress, 2003.

Laban. *In Jewish Encyclopedia Online.* Available: http://jewishencyclopedia.com/articles/9568-laban.

McKenzie, Steven L. 2 Samuel. In *Michael Coogan (ed.). The New Oxford Annotated Bible.* New York: Oxford University Press, 2010.

Matthews, Victor. *Manners and Customs in the Bible.* Peabody, MA: Hendrickson Publishers, 1988.

Moller, Karl. "Prophecy and Prophets in the Old Testament." In *Dictionary of Theological Interpretation.* Grand Rapids, MI: Baker Academic, 2005.

NIV Archaeological Study Bible. Grand Rapids, MI: Zondervan, 2005.

Porter, Jeanne. *Leading Ladies.* Minneapolis, MN: Augsburg Books, 2005.

Shanks, Hershel. *Ancient Israel.* Washington, DC: Prentice Hall and Biblical Archaeology Society, 1999.

Sharp, Carolyn. "What Is a Prophet?" In *Old Testament Prophets for Today.* Louisville, KY: Westminster John Knox Press, 2009.

Shewell-Cooper, W. E. "Mandrakes." In *GLO Premium Electronic Bible.* Orlando, FL: Immersion Digital, Inc., 2010

Shewell-Cooper, W. E. "Flax." In *Glo Bible Electronic Premium Edition.* Orlando, FL: Immersion Digital, Inc., 2010.

Ury, M. William. "Holiness." In B*aker Theological Dictionary of the Bible.* Grand Rapids, MI: Baker Books, 1996.

White, W. Jr. "Synagogue." In *Glo Bible Electronic Premium Edition.* Orlando, FL: Immersion Digital Inc., 2010.

Wright, Fred H. *Manners and Customs of Bible Lands.* Chicago: Moody Press, 1953.

Translations researched at biblegateway.com (accessed 3/8/2015).